THE NATURE OF BIRDS

THE NATURE OF BIRDS

ADRIAN FORSYTH

CAMDEN HOUSE

© Copyright 1988 by Camden House Publishing

Canadian Cataloguing in Publication Data

Forsyth, Adrian
    The nature of birds

ISBN 0-920656-65-X

1. Birds—Behaviour.   I. Title

QL698.3.F67 1988   598   C88-094516-8

Trade distribution by
Firefly Books
3520 Pharmacy Avenue, Unit 1-C
Scarborough, Ontario
Canada M1W 2T8

Printed in Canada for
Camden House Publishing
(a division of Telemedia Publishing Inc.)
7 Queen Victoria Road
Camden East, Ontario
K0K 1J0

Front Cover: Puffin, Bruce Lyon/Valan Photos

Back Cover: Leonard Rue Jr./DRK Photo

Designed by
Linda J. Menyes

Colour separations by
Hadwen Graphics Limited
Ottawa, Ontario

Printed and bound in Canada by
D.W. Friesen & Sons Ltd.
Altona, Manitoba

Printed on 80-lb. Jensen Gloss

ACKNOWLEDGMENTS

Many people have influenced my fascination with the lives of birds. I would like to mention the following as some who were of particular help to me on this project. Bruce Lyon, Michael Fogden and Patricia Fogden provided stimulating information and good company in the field. Bob Montgomerie helped keep me informed about new work in avian behavioural ecology. Patrick Weatherhead kindly read and corrected a draft of the book. And Turid Forsyth contributed in ways too numerous to credit.

A special thanks to my publisher Frank B. Edwards for his ongoing support, to my editor Tracy C. Read, who remained flexible about deadlines and skeptical about jargon, to art director Linda J. Menyes and to the Camden House copy department, Susan Dickinson, Patricia Denard-Hinch, Mary Patton, Catherine De Lury, Charlotte DuChene and Peggy Denard.

The use of the libraries and the librarians' time at Queen's University at Kingston and the Royal Ontario Museum are also gratefully acknowledged.

CONTENTS

NESTS
Deciphering the architecture of the avian empire
15

BEAUTY
High-profile plumage in a competitive world
29

SONG
Interpreting the nature of music
43

MATING
Reproductive success and the rites of spring
55

COLONIES
How birds benefit from the company they keep
73

PROPAGANDA
Whole truths, half truths and outright lies
87

IMAGES
Startled predators and disguised prey
97

INTELLIGENCE
The costs and benefits of having a brain
105

IGNOBLE NATURE
Infanticide, cuckoldry and other natural acts
113

RELATIONSHIPS
Odd couplings and the politics of parasitism
121

THE EMIGRANT FACTOR
A biologist's defence of a global perspective
135

BIRD WATCHING
Scholarship and fieldwork in the hands of amateurs
145

SOURCES
155

INDEX
157

Commonly found in watery habitats, egrets feed on fish, aquatic insects, grasshoppers and moths, and nest both singly and in colonies (left).

PREFACE

Each spring, groups of male sage grouse (left) gather on the plains to show off their fine plumage, puffing out their splendid white chests and spreading their spectacular tail feathers to attract a mate. Females visit these ritual leks only long enough to choose a partner; having mated, they depart to raise their young alone.

One winter, I spent a month tracking ruffed grouse. The weather cooperated, either by dusting the crust of snowpack with a light powder or by thawing just enough of it to record the tread of the foraging grouse. One grouse had a range conveniently close to my house, in an area open and flat enough for me to ski through, which allowed me to get a detailed impression of its meandering trails. Late in the day, that particular bird always headed toward the same fallen tree. The tree's upturned roots faced southwest, and the sun and eddying wind had melted out a protective hollow where the bird passed the night. The grouse displayed a penchant for serviceberry buds, and the daily routes it travelled to arrive at them were obscure and various. Heading across the fields on its way to the bush, it never roamed in a straight line. First, it struck out for a white birch. Plodding past the base of the tree, it then set out across the open toward a patch of prickly ash. At long last, after a tortuous zigzagging journey, the grouse reached its apparent goal. Even when the snow was wet or deep

enough to make walking difficult, the bird used the same method.

Another grouse, which lived in heavier forest nearby, did most of its foraging by simply flying up into the crown of a large ironwood tree and feeding on its buds. Those two birds, both of which lived in the same area, had radically different foraging techniques.

After giving their disparate methods some thought, I began to understand that each bird was behaving in a way which was appropriate to its special living conditions. The open-habitat bird travelled in a laborious fashion that, while metabolically expensive and time-consuming, served to reduce its exposure to predators such as hawks and great horned owls, which might spot it from above. The closed-forest grouse was free to take a more direct route to its feeding site.

Contemplating the reasons for particular behaviours is a large part of the pleasure I derive from nature. Once upon a time, everyone was a naturalist and was familiar with hundreds of plant species and their uses. They knew when a specific tree would

9

produce fruit and what kinds of animals and insects it would attract. They recognized the calls of birds and knew where and when they nested. But industrialization and the growth of urban centres have eclipsed that common wisdom; today's naturalists encounter formidable barriers in their attempts to interpret the natural world. While an enjoyment of the smells, sounds and sights of nature is fundamental, they will soon find that ideas are just as essential to their appreciation as field guides and binoculars. Nature challenges our minds as well as our senses, and exploring the connection between science and the human attempt to order our experience is the naturalist's most intriguing task.

The standard approach to bird study has been to set out with a field guide and begin to identify and name birds. Although that is an important first step, most people find it is not enough to hold their interest and go on to become birders, who pursue bird identification as a sport and social activity. Birding is often perceived by such people as a social event where they can also test themselves in a congenial manner, much as others

The long-necked, all-white trumpeter swan (above), renowned for its call that carries great distances over water, majestically displays its 10-foot wingspan. The Bonaparte's gull (right) takes great care in cleaning the barbs of its feathers with its bill. Because the ability to fly is so important to their survival, gulls remove oil and dirt from their feathers that could build up and hamper flight.

The immature goshawk feeding on a slain squirrel (top left) is getting an early start on a life of bloody predation. Well known for its habit of diving into the water from the air, the brown pelican (left) goes fishing in Florida. Snow geese (above) travel in large numbers to their Arctic nesting grounds, where population concentrations can reach more than 1,200 pairs per square mile.

gather to play golf. It is the company of fellow birders and the quest, as much as the birds themselves, that pique their interest.

An understanding of bird behaviour and natural history, though, gives the birder's quest new significance. The sighting of a cowbird becomes much more meaningful to those who know that it once grazed on the backs of buffalo and that it has had to cope with tremendous change—the clearing of the eastern forests for agriculture and the demise of the wild western bison herds. The knowledge that cowbird females lay their eggs in other birds' nests to escape the responsibility of rearing their nestlings prompts us to look at them differently.

These essays are about using ideas to comprehend the ecology of bird behaviour in particular and nature in general. They explore two main themes: first, that our experience determines what we are able to perceive and understand; and second, that such an understanding increases our appreciation of nature and our empathy with other organisms. They deal with topics of

special interest to me; I have not attempted a general survey. Instead, I have concentrated on themes that dominate the science of behavioural ecology—one of the fastest-growing areas of biology—which focuses on the relationship between ecology and the evolution of behaviour. It has radically changed our perception of the degree of sophistication that organisms such as birds bring to their behaviour.

Some of the concepts and arguments used in behavioural ecology are complex and convoluted. And since we are an animal that enjoys thinking, no apology or oversimplification is in order: nature is complex and convoluted.

I hope that the essays capture some of the intricacies of natural history and of the human reaction to nature. Unlike science, natural history does not labour under the yoke of objectivity. The naturalist's interaction with nature depends as much on experience, culture and beliefs as it does on factual knowledge. Natural history can be as complicated and as cryptic as we are.

13

NESTS

Deciphering the architecture of the avian empire

The screech owl tucked securely into the entrance of a hollow sycamore tree (left) has acquired a valuable ecological resource. Nest sites, especially well-protected cavities in trees, are often in short supply. Many individuals in cavity-nesting species fail to breed each year due to the lack of a cavity.

One May afternoon, after an unusually violent spring storm, I noticed a handful of debris lying on the woodshed roof below our kitchen window. I removed the window screen and stepped onto the roof for a closer look at the conglomeration of mud, moss and straw—a seemingly sodden mass of trash. At one time, I would have kicked the debris away. That day, however, I carefully carried what was in fact the nest of a barn swallow into the house to try to decipher its story.

There are palaeontologists who can reconstruct the figure of a dinosaur from a few fragments of bone, trackers who trace the history of a game herd using barely discernible markings on the ground and archaeologists who, by sifting through ancient garbage pits, re-create the lives of people who existed thousands of years ago. Perhaps we can do the same with birds' nests; after all, a nest is avian life history and behaviour made tangible.

Nest reading is merely a specialized example of a more general skill—the close scrutiny and abstract contemplation of simple objects. We begin the reading by observing and thinking selectively: What is the possible adaptive significance of a particular detail or design? What are the costs and benefits of its manufacture? How did it come to be as it is?

The swallow's nest contained plenty of mud, including a plane of adobe that had mortared it to the wall. The cost-and-benefit trade-offs of that design seemed obvious: mud is an economical, widely available building material that can be thrown on quickly without the time-consuming twisting of fibrous attachments. But the nest's fall from its graceful placement near the peak of our roof was evidence of mud's bonding limitations. The mud attachment may have been well suited to a stationary rock ledge; a wood-frame house, however, bends slightly under the force of a strong wind. The inflexible mud holdfasts had popped free of the flexing substrate.

When I began to think of both the swallow's use of mud and its selection of our gable as evolved adaptations, the nest itself conjured up an image of a suddenly transformed species and landscape. In the time of vast pre-Columbian forests, barn swallows must have been rather rare—wild, patchily distributed birds closely tied to cliff faces that rose from lakeshores and lined river canyons. Since then, the nest design has allowed the swallows to become ubiquitously abundant, almost domestic. And the arrival of European agriculturists precipitated the rapid conversion of barn swallows into a plebeian species, the common inhabitants of barnyards and highway bridges. Thus the muddy swallow's nest spoke to me not only of architectural design but also of numerical fortune gained at the expense of wildness.

Naturalists were not always equipped with the perspective of change, of mutable costs and benefits in design. One of my prized possessions is a massive tome on natural history published in 1823, when Charles Darwin was only 14 years old. The author, Simon Shaw, begins exuberantly, extolling the pleasures found in contemplating nature. When I read it, I am struck by how moribund the pre-Darwinian creationist view of the world is. Shaw believed that "the real state of every object illustrates the inconceivable omnipotence of the God of nature. The whole system of nature is a vast museum." Yet although Shaw's desire to read and understand nature was strong, his comments exude a hopelessness. "The primary cause of the most common existence," he laments, "we cannot comprehend."

Darwin, however, freed the contemplative naturalist from that static point of view. As a consequence, every natural object offers our imaginations a history and biography. Rather than simply admiring the nest as a work woven without hands, we wonder how it came here and what its future is. More importantly, we begin to realize that barn swallows have not been passive pawns of omnipotent creation. They have had a role in their own fate.

When I pulled apart the swallow's nest, I uncovered a saga of choices and options. The nest was made of mud mixed with straw

and moss, just as adobe is, to keep it from cracking. The proportions of the nest material did not suddenly come about: they resulted from the trial-and-error process of mutation and selection. Some swallows used cohesive, moist materials; some settled for mud that was gritty with sand; others used fine clay. Some chose only sturdy sites, such as the unshifting rock of a cliff face; others were more adventurous, settling in locations as precarious as an earthen escarpment.

Out of that long history—the selective winnowing of various behaviour patterns which differed in their success—comes the nest the naturalist finds. Although the details of its history are unverifiable, the pleasure of wondering why things are as they are is not diminished.

A Hot Little Machine

The most beautifully crafted nest I have ever seen is that of the female ruby-throated hummingbird. A classic cup-shaped construction set on top of a branch, the nest is primarily fine moss woven together with spider webbing. Its centre is lined with delicate down teased from assorted plant fibres, while the outer layer is embellished, and thereby camouflaged, with grey-green *Parmelia* lichens carefully distributed over the upper surface. The finished nest is ornately trimmed, as though it has been carefully decorated to suit human aesthetic sensibility. But I suspect it follows its own adaptive script.

The thickness and finely woven interior of the cup are among its remarkable features; it has none of the loose, straggly quality of many nests. So much material is packed into the cup that there is little room left for the female that builds the nest. The cup is unusually deep, almost uncomfortably so—sitting on her eggs, the ruby-throat is nearly out of view; only her head and long tail protrude above the rim.

It is tempting to attribute the fine weave and the artful placement of the nest to the hummingbird's delicate and dexterous bill, which more closely resembles an embroidery needle or a loom shuttle than it does most bird beaks. My guess, however, is that

the ultimate function of the nest's depth and elegance is related to the hummingbird's small size and high metabolism. The hummingbird is a hot little machine whose heart beats a thousand times per minute and whose body temperature is near 105 degrees F. But neither the bird nor its eggs have much thermal mass for retaining heat or buffering the incubation process against fluctuations in air temperature. It is difficult for a hummingbird to store enough energy to maintain its body temperature through the night, and it often slips into a lower-temperature torpor, a mild kind of overnight hibernation, to reduce energy consumption. A hummingbird's temperature during the night is usually 70 degrees higher than that of the air, even in warm climates. I have found the nests of tropical-forest hummingbirds to be as finely made and as well insulated as those of our hardy temperate ruby-throats.

It follows that the hummingbird's small size makes a highly insulated nest something of a necessity. On the other hand, perhaps its nest-building skills enabled it to evolve its tiny body size. In all likelihood, the two trends developed in concert. But since the ruby-throat is a recent resident of the north, I suspect that the key adaptation of its nest was originally related not to insulation but, rather, to its evolution in the predator-rich Tropics.

Hummingbirds use orb-weaving spiders as a source of food and construction materials. I often see them plucking both the spiders and their entangled prey from the webs. Delicate bills and hovering flight allow them to gather large quantities of spider silk. The lightness and strength of the fibre, in turn, enables tropical hummingbirds to situate their nests in protected spots at the tips of bamboo spikes or on the ends of palm fronds or dangling banana leaves. The hummingbird's use of spider silk may have allowed the bird to create the compact, densely insulated nests it needs in colder climates. Perhaps selection for nest placement in the Latin American rain forests has made it possible for me to watch ruby-throats in Ontario; the weave and tangles of

The nest of this female broad-tailed hummingbird (above) is a deep, thick-walled cup woven of fine plant fibres and spider webbing. The nest design provides good thermal insulation, thereby minimizing the loss of the female's body heat and improving its ability to incubate its clutch. Both the male and the female cliff swallows (right) work at building their flask-shaped nest. Hundreds of pellets of mud are plastered together to create a structure that can be mounted on any stable vertical surface—a cliff, a barn wall or an embankment. This style of construction enables swallows to place their nests beyond the reach of most terrestrial predators.

17

ultimate result of this unique trend is the Asian cave swift, whose cup-shaped nest consists entirely of salivary glue. The bird's-nest soup sought by aficionados of Asian cuisine is based on these masses of solidified swift spittle.

Inevitably, there are potential costs and benefits of such alternative designs. Saliva lacks the insulating features of fine plant fibres, and as a result, swift eggs, at least those of the common swift that nests in the temperate climate of Europe, have evolved a high degree of resistance to chilling. As well, the salivary secretions enable the birds to build beyond the reach of predators.

Predators are the harshest and most important judges of nest construction and placement. Skill in siting is always an integral part of a nest's story, so it helps to think like a predator when looking at the positioning of a nest. When I find a northern oriole nest dangling far out on the end of a birch limb, I have an account of the forces that must influence these birds.

First, I am impressed by how the oriole female exploits the range of fibre and flexibility in native plants. She weaves strands of the graceful lakeside Indian hemp *Apocynum cannabinum*, just as the original human inhabitants of eastern Ontario—the Huron, Algonquin and Iroquois—used them for rope and fishnets. Whenever I see oriole nests, I wonder whether the first human wanderers reaching the east of the New World independently discovered that *Apocynum* hemp could be woven or whether someone watched a female northern oriole peel the fraying stalks and rope her basket to a twig.

Milkweed fluff from old seedpods is also twisted into rope by the oriole, and its pewter-coloured strands run all around the basket. The heart of the construction is a felt made from the ragged brown skin of river grapes. Along the opening rim, white-pine needles and slivers of split cedarwood are inserted to join the interior to the padded base, thus creating a structured form. The lining consists of animal hair coiled round and round until it stays in a neat, tight circle with no loose ends.

the ruby-throat's nest span continents and aeons and bind spiders, snakes and the larger world to the tiny hovering bird.

Shared Ancestry

One of the best ways to appreciate a particular species is to compare its features with those exhibited by genetically similar birds, a comparison that is especially illuminating when the two relatives are products of distinctly different ecologies. Swifts and hummingbirds are closely related, but ecologically, swifts are more like swallows. Swifts have developed nest-building techniques that attest to both their shared ancestry with hummingbirds and their swallowlike foraging habits. They evolved into sociable, short-billed, fleet-winged sailing birds that need open spaces. Like swallows, they feed on clouds of insects and often nest in colonies on cliffs, banks, towers and isolated trees that are perfectly suited to their freewheeling flight.

Some species perch on ledges in accessible locations. That is the habit of the black swift, which nests in western North and Central America from Alaska to Costa Rica; using its minimal nest-building skills, it assembles its mossy cup on cliff ledges or on the rock faces behind waterfalls. The

white-throated swift prefers a dry habitat and has a more highly evolved nest-building technique: it uses a gluelike secretion from its specialized salivary glands to fasten its cup-shaped structure to a seam high on a cliff face. The chimney swift—the only swift that nests east of the Mississippi—perhaps enjoys a broader range because of its willingness to settle in structures as ubiquitous as hollow tree trunks. It, too, secretes a viscous substance to bind an assemblage of sticks. But the tropical American palm swift is the most skilled constructor of all, gluing together a bag-shaped structure to hang from palm leaves.

When we compare the shared features of swallows and swifts, we see their ecologically convergent element. Both build on tall structures in open habitats suited to their practice of foraging colonially for aerial insects, yet they achieve that similar siting through different methods. The fact that many swifts construct their nests primarily with plant material, rather than soil, seems attributable to their common ancestry with hummingbirds, which also use plant material. But each group has its own special abilities. Unlike hummingbirds, swifts have evolved a unique method of holding their nests together: they use salivary glue. The

The shy red-necked grebe (far left) usually builds its nest far from the shoreline of a marsh, in an area with water several feet deep. The nest is a floating island piled into a mound and anchored by attaching material to a rooted reed or cattail. By tearing strips from a palm leaf, the hooded oriole (left) makes its own supply of fine fibres. The strands of palm leaf are flexible and strong and are suitable for weaving and suspending the cup nest from slender branches and leaves beyond the reach of most climbing predators. The nest of the male African grosbeak weaver (above) displays the fine weaving skills typical of many African weaver birds. The adaptive significance of a nest woven to two thin cattail stalks that would not support most conventional cup nests may be related to the presence of sophisticated egg-eating snakes and many climbing and egg-eating primates in Africa. Like the orioles of the New World, the African weavers can place their nests in hard-to-reach places.

After my initial burst of admiration for the artistic use of natural materials, I again muse on the function of the pendulous swinging basket. Serving as much more than a cradle for eggs and nestlings, the design seems to be an attempt to reach that valuable predator-free space, beyond the reach of the dexterous hands of such mammals as raccoons. The oriole basket hangs out of reach of all but the lightest nest robbers—only squirrels and snakes are likely to get to it.

That does not mean the oriole has hit upon an ideal nest design; all adaptations limit an organism in some way. The basket may reduce nest predation, but it is ill-suited to windy sites and closed-canopy forest. The northern oriole is limited to an existence as a forest-edge species because of its need to search out high, isolated limbs. A consid-

Like other gulls, the Arctic tern (top left) has a nest that is little more than a depression in the ground. Nesting usually takes place colonially, and terrestrial predators are vigorously mobbed en masse. The relatively precocial tern chicks, which are born with eyes open and some feather down, do not depend on a nest for protection or insulation. Altricial nestlings, born blind, helpless and unable to regulate their body temperatures, like the red-winged blackbird nestlings (above), remain several weeks in the cup nest and depend on it as a haven against predators. The cup nest of silvery milkweed fibres woven by yellow warblers (left) is a generalized nest architecture which enables yellow warblers to nest in a greater range of habitat types than bird species that employ more elaborate and specialized nest design. Each year, the finely built nest is discarded and a new nest woven, perhaps as a means of avoiding a buildup of parasitic mites and insects.

eration of constraints and compromises reveals what is important to a bird species and what is not.

Tropical orioles also take into account arboreal nest robbers by choosing their neighbours carefully, preferring to nest in association with colonies of social wasps such as *Stelopolybia.* I know from painful experience that the hornets are armed with a barbed, venomous sting much like that of the honeybee. Vibration of the branch on which the colony's nest hangs sends hundreds of workers swarming out to attack the intruder. A variation of this tactic is employed by a species of tropical flycatcher that is mysteriously able to nest in acacia trees totally infested with *Pseudomyrmex* ants. These ants are the bane of dry tropical forest in Central America. Merely brushing an ant-infested acacia tree sends the insects rushing over your body, and they are uncannily adept at thrusting their stingers into the tenderest, most nerve-rich areas. Although I do not know how the flycatchers reach a mutual understanding with the ants,

the value of such a nest site is obvious.

The nasty-neighbour strategy is not strictly a tropical phenomenon: many northern and temperate birds site their nests near an aggressive neighbouring bird. Arctic tern colonies, for example, attract old-squaw ducks that probably benefit from the terns' willingness to mob intruding predators. Biologist Karen Clark and ecologist Raleigh Robertson conducted a study that looked at yellow warblers' tendency to nest in loose aggregations with other species. They found that warblers nesting near catbirds suffered less predation and that those nesting near red-winged blackbirds sustained less brood parasitism from cowbirds dumping their eggs in the warbler nests.

My own experience reinforces their findings. When I give my crude imitation of the "pish pish pish" mobbing call used by North American songbirds, one bird that frequently shows up is the catbird. Large and exhibiting a defensive demeanour, the catbird does a good job of fending off squirrels and other intruders. The redwing is also an alert nest defender, especially against cowbirds; I have placed model cowbirds near redwing colonies, and the redwings soon batter them to pieces.

In autumn, when the leaves fall, yellow warbler nests are so plentiful in the thickets of spiraea, red osier and prickly ash that I have always assumed the warblers wove them wherever they could find an unoccupied space. Now, I must admit that their choice of nest sites is based on ecological forces of which I have only a glimmer of awareness.

The abundance of warblers' nests raises a question about their disposable nature. Given that most nests are durable enough to survive a winter and, with a small amount of repair, would be serviceable the following spring, why are they abandoned? The same question can be asked about the finely woven nests of the oriole, which often last for several years.

Some songbirds, such as the eastern phoebe, do reuse their nests; I suspect that the reason is historical. Phoebes, like barn swallows, were once rare, and their pres-

superior construction materials; however, much of the material was added after the nest structure was built and the eggs had been laid. It appeared, then, that the birds were, in effect, selecting aromatic plants which might repel or destroy nest parasites. And when the chosen plants were tested, they were found to impede the growth of lice and bacteria.

That study made me realize I had been taking much for granted about the materials birds use in the construction of their nests. I had assumed that convenience and structural features like strength and flexibility were the important considerations. I was well aware of both the problem of nest parasites and the fact that the green world of plants is actually a complex realm of thousands of chemical molecules used for defence against insects. But I never imagined that birds might have evolved a means of exploiting the plants' chemical defence as a nest-sanitation strategy.

Since ornithologists have become aware of the possibility that nests may be chemically designed, several interesting findings have emerged. A survey of North American raptors revealed that the species which add sprigs of greenery to their nests during breeding are usually those which also reuse them. Some of the nests have become massive accumulations of sticks, bones, feathers and offal suitable for breeding pest populations. There is a record of a bald eagle nest that was active for 36 years; since new material is added annually, their nests can grow to a depth of six yards.

Eastern screech owls employ an even more aggressive antiparasite practice: they bring live blind snakes to their nests to feed on the parasites. F.R. Gehlbach and R.S. Baldridge of Baylor University, in Texas, observed that while screech owls normally decapitate snakes and carry them dangling and dead back to their nest cavities, blind snakes were transported alive, coiled conveniently around the owls' bills. Fourteen of the screech owl nest boxes harboured live blind snakes in the nest debris. Normally, blind snakes live in ant and termite colonies, where they feed on the soft-bodied larval

ence was confined to cave openings and overhanging rock ledges, sites that necessitated a durable nest designed for repeated use. But phoebes are an exception; nest reuse by cup nesters is uncommon. When it does occur, it seems to be profitable inasmuch as the time-energy savings are translated into increased reproductive success. In one study of eastern phoebes, birds that reused nests had larger clutches than birds that built their nests from scratch.

I once got a firsthand demonstration of why reusing old nests is infrequent among songbirds. Phoebes had been nesting on an electrical outlet in our woodshed for several years, gradually enlarging the nest and eventually encrusting the fixture. Finally, when the current crop had fledged, I decided to liberate the fixture. I pulled the nest loose and had a look at it. A second later, I dropped it, horrified at the sight of a purple-grey legion of lice seething off the nest and rampaging across my hand.

Birds' nests attract a rich host of scavengers, predators of the scavengers and ectoparasites that feed on the nestlings and adults. The latter group consists of assorted lice, fleas, bedbugs, assassin bugs, mites and flies, and a nest may contain dozens of species and thousands of individuals. The

concerted action of all of the nest parasites combined with the high probability of blood diseases apparently make it more profitable for most birds to construct a new nest each year. The cost of nest parasites is sometimes outweighed by other considerations. Birds that reuse nests include cavity nesters and certain raptors, and competition for sites may predispose them to do so. Starlings, for example, compete fiercely for nest cavities, whether used or not, and have evolved a remarkable set of behaviours that seem to discourage nest parasites.

The starling is just one bird that adds green vegetation to its nest. The adaptive significance of the behaviour has been tested by Larry Clark and Russ Mason of the Monell Chemical Senses Center in Philadelphia. They began by asking whether starlings are selective about the plants they use or whether they gather plants at random from the nest area. By surveying the relative abundance of the different plant species in the area and comparing it with those found in the nests, Clark and Mason determined that starlings were selective, actively seeking out pungent herbs such as yarrow and agrimony and tending to ignore plants such as dandelions. One possible explanation is that the chosen plants simply constitute

A female ornate hawk-eagle (far left) has returned to its nest of dry sticks high on a Guatemalan ceiba tree carrying a sprig of foliage from another plant, a habit which is common for raptors that reuse their nests over many years. Evidence suggests that some birds improve nest sanitation by choosing leaves containing insecticidal or antibacterial compounds. The Harris's hawk, found in southwestern areas of the United States, often nests on a cactus (above), a nest site that offers built-in protection against most climbing predators. Broad-winged hawks (right) often use an old crow nest as a base for their nesting platform, which saves them considerable time and energy. In turn, the nests of raptors may be reused by species such as great horned owls, which never build their own.

and immature life stages. In the screech owl nests, they consume blowfly maggots. An experiment that compared nests with and without snakes found the daily growth rate of the owl nestlings to be faster when the snakes were present, implying a clear benefit in having live snakes around. It may seem somewhat farfetched, but it is hardly more unlikely than many other well-known but bizarre relationships between species.

Natural Repellents

Another method of repelling predators is with physical and chemical barriers. Indian house sparrows have a penchant for leaves from the neem tree, a plant that produces a potent natural insecticide. The repellent defence is highly developed by the red-cockaded woodpeckers of the southeastern pine forests, which nest in holes excavated in living trees. The woodpeckers open the tree bark to let the sap and protective compounds seep out, and they remain interested in a tree only as long as it continues to yield sap. The sticky pine gum accumulates below and around the nest entrance and acts primarily as a barrier against rat snakes, which are superb tree climbers.

I am continually amazed at the sight of a black rat snake going up a two-foot-diameter tree trunk, a girth far too large for the snake to coil around. Rat snakes use special belly scales to wedge and lever against the bark fissures, which allows them to ascend vertically, not unlike rock climbers who move up a cliff face by wedging bolts and digits into a network of cracks and crevices. The same technique allows rat snakes to gain access to protected tree cavities, where they can coil in safety for the exhausting process of shedding their skin. Their climbing ability also allows them access to many birds' nests, but they are foiled by the red-cockaded woodpecker's impenetrable sticky gum barrier.

A variation of the technique has been independently evolved by the red-breasted nuthatch, which frequents more northerly coniferous forests. It collects dabs of pine gum to smear around the nest-hole entrance, a tactic that is probably directed not

so much at snakes as at other cavity-nesting birds, small rodents and possibly biting insects which may be repelled by both the tacky quality of the resin and its powerful terpenic odour.

The white-breasted nuthatch performs the same rite with different materials. It may stuff mammal fur into bark crevices or pick up a beetle, such as a meloid blister beetle, and wipe it back and forth against the bark near the nest. When molested, meloids exude a yellow secretion of acrid cantharidin compounds from their leg joints. Having been burned by the ooze, I can testify to its noxious nature. The nuthatch's use of such insects presumably repels nest robbers like squirrels and chipmunks, which are able to locate nests, eggs and nestlings by following scent trails.

Naturalists have been puzzled by the ex-

citement the great crested flycatcher displays over snakeskins. A cavity nester, the flycatcher weaves the skin into the rim of its nest, dangling part of it out of the entrance. The most obvious explanation for such behaviour is that it has evolved because it works — nest-robbing jays and squirrels are duped into believing that the cavity is occupied by a large rat snake.

In his Peterson *Field Guide to Birds' Nests*, Hal Harrison claims the idea is unacceptable, arguing that the bird probably does not recognize a snakeskin as such and that tufted titmice also habitually use snakeskins. But whether or not the bird recognizes the snakeskin is irrelevant. If its inclusion in the nest somehow dissuades nest-robbing birds and squirrels, the behaviour will be favoured by natural selection. It is also worth noting that tufted titmice and

Unlike many cavity-nesting birds, woodpeckers, such as the pileated woodpecker (far left), are able to excavate their own nest site. Most other cavity nesters, like bluebirds or tree swallows, occupy the woodpecker nest after the woodpeckers have abandoned it and moved on to excavate a new cavity. Even a rotted-out knothole is enough to attract a screech owl (above), which adds no nesting material and simply requires a secure site for its offspring. The demand for nest and roost sites is so intense that the owl will also use artificial nest boxes, which facilitates the study of cavity nesters and makes it possible to rebuild populations in areas where the dead and so-called "overmature" trees have been logged out.

chickadees disturbed in their nest cavities open their mouths and hiss as they move from side to side, in a clear imitation of the threat display of snakes. Their behaviour further supports the idea that the snakeskin may be a useful ploy. The theory, which I call the talisman hypothesis, remains just that, a speculative hypothesis. But it is one that any naturalist with access to rat snakes and squirrels could easily test.

I mention Harrison's skepticism because it bears on an important aspect of how we develop our understanding and appreciation of birds' nests and the birds that build them. The adaptationist believes that the way organisms look and behave reflects selective pressures acting on them and that we can detect design in nature. Those who naïvely accept that every creature and trait are perfectly designed ignore the historical origins of traits. Phoebes, for example, will line the rafters of a shed with nest after empty nest because they either cannot count or cannot remember which of the uniformly spaced beams is home. They are simply not adapted for this novel environment.

Adaptation is a dynamic historical process, the constant modification of an organism in response to the demands of its environment and ecology. The adaptive fit between what an organism does or looks like and the difficulties and opportunities it faces is never fixed or perfect. Nevertheless, when we walk in nature, it is the adaptationist perspective that helps us first explore a phenomenon. If we assume that snakeskins appear regularly in crested flycatcher nests simply because the skin is conveniently long and pliable or that live blind snakes in owl nests are there only by accident, then we learn nothing new.

We set out on the road to understanding nature by asking questions: Does this behaviour have any possible adaptive significance? What benefit might the bird be receiving from it? What are the trade-offs? Our various explanations may be proved wrong. Snakeskins might not repel nest robbers, and blind snakes might simply be confusingly difficult for a screech owl to kill because it is hard to distinguish which end

is head and which is tail. In our efforts to find the answers, we must be careful to avoid underestimating the biological sophistication of birds.

Anthropologist and essayist Loren Eiseley wrote about the meaning of the golden hieroglyphic markings on a cone shell he had found while beachcombing. The markings were no more and no less than the mindless writing of mollusk glands, but Eiseley called them "the golden alphabet." The mollusk bore the name *Conus spurious*, an appellation Eiseley considered unjustified because, as he put it, "the golden alphabet, in whatever shape it chooses to reveal itself, is never spurious. From its inscrutable lettering is created man and all the streaming cloudland of his dreams."

A reading of the golden alphabet begins with our paying homage to simple things. Eiseley's cone shell and the humble barnswallow nest are no less than the handiwork of thousands of years of evolutionary tinkering and refinement. That is why there are fundamental messages in even the simplest natural objects. We live in a time when evolutionary rules are being discovered; they are the grammar of the golden alphabet and will help us to interpret the messages on shells and in the mud of a swallow's nest.

The stick platform of the female anhinga (above) has a crude appearance, but it is an economical construction that serves its purpose by supporting the two heavy chicks. The simple form matches its simple function. The need to radiate heat explains the flimsy nest structure of the nest of the white-winged dove (right). In the heat of the desert, where daytime temperatures are often above 104 degrees F, investing in a well-insulated nest is unnecessary. Indeed, the need to radiate body heat explains the flimsy nest structure; nothing more than what is needed to contain the eggs and nestlings is used.

BEAUTY

High-profile plumage in a competitive world

The massive fan spread by the male peacock (left) is an attention-arresting array of iridescent eyespots surrounding the electric-blue chest and throat. While the fan is attractive to peahens, its awkwardness reduces the male's ability to evade predators.

Behind our house is a shady section of forest and stream, much used by mammals and songbirds. The trees are a mix of sugar maple, sweet birch, blue beech and hazel, and the soil is black and thriving with shrews and worms. The stream breeds an abundance of insects and cuts a corridor through the forest, a busy conduit for birds, flies and water snakes. As I dawdled there one day in June, mesmerized by the fast-moving water eddying around my boots, a male scarlet tanager suddenly settled in the water.

Oblivious to my presence, it splashed vigorously in the shallows where a shaft of sunlight played on a riffle. Its brilliant scarlet body and gleaming black wings flickering in a golden spray seemed to burn amid the sombre green surroundings. I watched, riveted by the beauty of the shimmering, glowing bird.

What was it that made the tanager so captivating? In my thirst for more of that beauty, I have tried to understand its origins by pondering such questions as, Why are some birds more beautiful than others? and

What is beauty? It was Darwin who made the most comprehensive attempt ever to answer these questions.

Humans are well equipped to respond to the aesthetic aspect of birds: we see many of the same colours as do birds, our eardrums quiver to similar sounds. Our shared physiology allows us to appreciate their beauty with our eyes and ears. Darwin observed that "birds seem to be the most aesthetic of all animals, excepting, of course, man, and they have nearly the same taste for the beautiful as we have. This is shown by our enjoyment of the singing of birds and by our women, both civilized and savage, decking their heads with borrowed plumes and using gems which are hardly more brilliantly coloured than the naked skin and wattles of certain birds."

The elaborate displays and ornaments of the birds that we find beautiful puzzled Darwin. Observing that such characteristics decreased a male's ability to survive and feed by rendering it conspicuous to predators and by impeding its movement, he

29

Bright colours act as beacons for visual predators. The sharp-shinned hawk standing on the yellow chest of a freshly killed meadowlark (above) may have been attracted by its conspicuous plumage. The male goldfinch perched in a winterberry tree (far right) has lost its gaudy gold summer colour and adopted a mousy brown winter plumage. The brilliant feathers flaunted during courtship become a liability once they have achieved their purpose.

wondered how natural selection had brought about the evolution of flashy, vulnerable males. He argued that the answer was to be found in the process of "sexual selection." Those same gaudy characteristics, he suggested, might enable a beautified male to sire more offspring than would an unadorned male. Sexual selection, therefore, was a special kind of natural selection. The value of sexual selection as a concept rested in the acknowledgment that evolutionary success depended not simply on the creature's ability to survive, find food and evade predators but also on its talent for acquiring mates either through effective courtship or by defeating reproductive rivals.

Sexual selection often causes one sex (usually the male) to evolve structures, colours and displays that are useful in attract-

ing a mate but decrease an individual's ability to survive. The colourful plumage of a male bird normally develops when it reaches sexual maturity, and the increased brightness is used in warning displays directed at male rivals and, with some species, in attracting females. A male is often able to interest more than one female and thereby maximize reproductive success. This is especially true in species whose males do not participate in the rearing of offspring. If a male's success is measured by the ability to attract mates, then males with beautiful plumage earn a genetic premium during mating season.

The same line of reasoning explains the dullness of female plumage. A female profits by rearing as large and as healthy a clutch of nestlings as possible. Mate attraction is not usually a major selective force on females because virtually all females in a population are mated each breeding season; there is no shortage of male suitors. On the other hand, there are many males in most bird populations that are unable to hold a territory or to attract females, which means that a few males obtain multiple matings, while some males do not mate at all.

But males pay a price for beauty. No hawk could fail to spot such birds as the male goldfinch, scarlet tanager and painted bunting when they are arrayed in their bold breeding plumages. Clear evidence of the cost of male beauty can be seen by noting the seasonal changes in male plumages. The male scarlet tanager or goldfinch, for instance, quickly reverts from its brilliant colours to a cryptic femalelike plumage after the mating period.

Increased predation is not the only cost of beauty. More prosaic aspects of life, such as feeding, may also be impaired by sexual selection. Boat-tailed grackles, for example, exhibit sexual dimorphism in tail and body size: the males' enlarged tails are used for sexual display. R.K. Selander, an evolutionary biologist interested in sexual selection, has shown that male grackles pay for the devices designed to enhance their mating success; their large, rudderlike tails and heavy bodies make them clumsy. Females glide gracefully over the water, plucking up insects from the surface. Males are too ungainly to take advantage of this rich food source. Selander also found that males suffer a higher mortality rate over the winter. The population of newly fledged grackles that he studied contained roughly equal numbers of males and females both at hatch and throughout the autumn; but by spring, males represented only 29 percent of the population.

The window in the room where I write looks out on a serviceberry tree. In June, the tree's crop of berries blushes waxy red and attracts goldfinches. Unless I concentrate and watch for quick, erratic movements, I scarcely notice the females; their muted colours blend with the foliage. Yet the colours of the males proclaim their presence.

Even when I am not looking directly at the tree, the golds and blacks register in my peripheral vision, and my eyes are irresistibly drawn to the small birds.

Witnessed in passing, the beauty of a male goldfinch is just light that dances across our retinas, firing cone cells as it goes. But it becomes more than mere light when the consequences of its brilliance are understood. I think of the bright gold feathers suddenly struck and pinned by the talons of a sharp-shinned hawk. Then I look again. The birds in the serviceberry tree are livelier now. They pluck a berry and stand alert. And if they seem more vibrantly alive, it is because death stands closer to them, its dark background enhancing their beauty.

Harmonic Movement

Most discussions about beauty revolve around 18th-century philosopher David Hume's notion that "beauty in things exists in the mind that contemplates them." It is my view that the natural world became more profoundly beautiful after Darwin's revelations. Here is another example of how the sense of beauty can grow with knowledge.

While driving into town last January, I was struck by the sight of pigeons lifting from a field. Bunched tightly together, they were more densely and precisely spaced than pigeon flocks I have seen in the city. The birds wheeled and dipped as one, in a beautiful display of coordinated formation flying. A second later, I saw the impetus for their meticulous harmonic movement: a snow-white gyrfalcon had sailed off a nearby barn roof and swooped down alongside the flock. But not a pigeon wavered. Turning as a unit, both falcon and flock sailed out of view.

Evolutionary biologist W.D. Hamilton's paper "Geometry for the Selfish Herd" described the phenomenon of flocking and herd formation as a consequence of individuals trying to minimize their chances of being picked off by a predator. The errant pigeon and the loosely scattered flock are attacked without mercy by raptors: the wages of sloppiness are death. Knowing that, I was more keenly conscious of the

necessary precision of the flock. Pathos suffused the pigeons' elegant spacing and created a richer kind of beauty.

Darwin's theory of sexual selection forced other naturalists to consider the proposition that animals other than ourselves possess a sense of beauty. He argued that sexual selection often operates through female choice of some males over other males, and he compared the role of female choice to the selection by animal breeders of particular aesthetic features. He wrote that "it appears that female birds in a state of nature have, by a long selection of the more attractive males, added to their beauty or other attractive qualities. No doubt this

implies powers of discrimination and taste on the part of the female which will, at first, appear extremely improbable, but . . . I hope to be able to show that the females actually have these powers."

The idea that female birds evaluate male displays is perfectly acceptable to me, as it probably is to most other naturalists. Anyone who has watched cowbirds on a lawn in spring has seen the males burbling, spreading their wings and dragging themselves around in front of the females, which refuse many an advance before agreeing to copulate. Female choice has also been demonstrated experimentally by biologists. A group of researchers at the University of

New Mexico has looked in detail at the red jungle fowl, the precursor of the domestic chicken. In carefully controlled experiments, they found that female jungle fowl were attracted to specific attributes of roosters. Females preferred males with large combs, redder hackle feathers and more golden saddle feathers; they were indifferent to the colour of the eyes and wattles, the length of the tail feathers and the male's size.

Darwin's friend and contemporary Alfred Russell Wallace refused to accept the possibility that female animals possessed an aesthetic sense by which they evaluated male beauty, perhaps believing that a capacity for evaluation presupposed consciousness. Wallace, a great naturalist and the codiscoverer of natural selection, disagreed with Darwin about the importance of sexual selection, claiming that male birds are brighter simply because of their inherently greater "male vigour." Such an argument is an example of a closed hypothesis. It assumes that there is such a thing as male vigour, which females lack. As such, it can never be tested or disproved.

By contrast, the Darwinian method is to ask, instead, How does beauty affect the reproductive fortunes of the males and females that possess it? By far, the most sophisticated example linking beauty and re-

Migrating redwings fly in dense flocks (left) in a display of synchronized flight that reduces the risk of aerial attack by falcons. The beauty of the peacock's feathers (above) is an adaptation favoured by sexual selection, wherein the rewards for conspicuous displays are deemed greater than the need for concealment from predators.

productive success in the animal world can be found in the bowerbirds of New Guinea. To attract females, the males build bowers on the ground that vary in complexity from species to species. They range from the simplest structures, which are merely cleared areas decorated with leaves, to complicated configurations of sticks—some in the form of erect towers, others with arching stick walls that form an avenue.

The most elaborate construction known to ornithologists is built by the Vogelkop bowerbird in the isolated mountains of Indonesian New Guinea. The bower is created around a sapling that supports a tower of sticks glued together with a salivary secretion. The edifice is more than six feet high. Sometimes, there are several towers, and in a few populations, the tower is built in the shape of a roofed hut with an open interior. A woven moss mat is laid out around the tower in a nearly perfect circle several yards in diameter. The mat and tower are decorated with natural objects that have been collected and arranged around the bower.

Ornithologist Thomas Gillard recorded the astonishing contents of various Vogelkop bowers. His notes for Nest Number 2 itemize the decorations: "A red cherry-sized fruit, a pile of small red seeds and fruits, a spray of vividly red fruits, piles of wilted applelike fruits (originally rose-red), a tall heap of 100 scarlet-orange flowers, one large yellow leaf, a pile of 40 green plum-sized fruits, a pile of 700 blue fruits, a pile of small blue fruits, a pile of 60 wilted brown plum-sized fruits, glistening brown resin, a black beetle skeleton, a black stick with 10 pieces of white funguslike substance."

In species such as the satin bowerbird or the Vogelkop bowerbird, the male, using a piece of bark as a brush and charcoal and saliva as the pigment, actually paints part of the bower. Other species use the juices from crushed leaves or fruit as paint. The male diligently tends to its ornaments, re-arranging, adding to and removing some of them daily. By placing objects such as coloured poker chips in the area, biologist Jared Diamond of the University of Califor-

nia, Los Angeles, has established that individuals and species show an incredible variation in creative style.

Within this system, the male is cast as artist, while the female's role is that of art critic. The bowerbird female tours a variety of bowers and judges the male's suitability by its skills in bower construction. If she finds the bower sufficiently attractive, the female then copulates with the male. The bower literally serves no other function than to assist the female in her choice of mate. Once mated, she leaves the male and proceeds to build a nest and raise her offspring alone.

The diversity in the artwork of different bowerbird species is a clear indication of how female choice serves to modify male appearance. As Gillard points out, the species with the dullest male plumage are also those that build the most elaborate bowers, while the species in which males have bright crests or other ornamentation build relatively simple bowers. This observation has led Gillard to suggest that during the evolutionary process, female choice for beautiful male appearance has been transferred progressively to the bower.

Evolutionary biologist Gerald Borgia has conducted studies of the satin bowerbird in

Lauterbach's bowerbird males arrange brightly coloured fruits around their woven bower of vegetation (above). The ornate arrangement, which is ultimately inspected and judged by females, may be rearranged daily by the male. The bower is not a nest; it is simply a creative act of courtship. Although males are typically more ornamented than females, both sexes of the African crowned crane (right) are equally flamboyant, a characteristic of monogamous birds in which both sexes engage in strong social-dominance interactions with other members of the same sex.

cicadas on their bowers were the most successful in winning the sexual attentions of visiting females and presumably fathered most of the next generation.

Cosmetic Defence

A bird's response to beauty may simply be its propensity to mate when confronted by an artistic and colourful display; no one need imagine that the decisions are conscious. But since female choice of beautiful males clearly does occur in various species, biologists have begun to ask why bright and colourful males are preferred in some species but not in others. Half a century ago, geneticist Ronald Fisher argued that many elaborate male characteristics might simply be the result of a female attraction to a male trait that was initially valuable as an indicator of, for example, health or genetic quality. The female attraction itself could then become the focus of sexual selection. As a result, males became more flamboyant simply because that flamboyance attracted females. And if the features of the successful males could be inherited, the females choosing these males would in turn produce the most colourful male offspring. The process would then favour the continued evolution of whatever male traits the average female found most attractive, and males would evolve to be more brilliant or to sing more impressively simply because these traits attracted females.

Yet such an argument does not address the question of why females were attracted to the bright male in the first place. Why did that particular preference evolve? Other biologists have speculated that females do, in fact, choose beautiful males for a reason. Evolutionary biologists W.D. Hamilton and Marlene Zuk suggest that females may select brightly coloured males whenever disease resistance is ecologically important. Pointing out that a poultry inspector can often visually assess the health of a bird and identify a specific disease by the appearance of its combs, wattles and plumage, Hamilton and Zuk theorize that female choice might favour males which advertise their health and freedom from disease

New South Wales, Australia, where young males essentially become apprentices to the craft of bower construction. Initial attempts are crude and usually undecorated. The male bowerbird visits the bowers of other males and observes them, taking several years to develop the skills necessary to create a complicated bower. Consequently, the female that selects a beautiful bower will be mating with a male which has survived for years and is competitive with other males, probably ensuring the female a mate that is relatively free from genetic defects and communicable diseases. In this sense, the beauty of the bower provides the female with adaptively useful information.

Borgia also found that a male's artistic ability affected its reproductive success. Males displaying the greatest number of blue feathers, coloured leaves and dead

through these characteristics. Since bird species differ in their susceptibility to viruses, bacteria, malaria and other parasites, the suggestion is that the males of species most at risk should aggressively advertise their health because females of the species would be strongly selected to mate with disease-free males.

Like most people, I reacted with skepticism when I initially read Hamilton and Zuk's research. It was difficult to believe that female choice based on male health and apparent disease resistance could result in the evolution of a cosmetic defence by males seeking to avoid being perceived as unhealthy. However, an independent study by Andrew Read of Oxford University shows that the most beautiful species were also those species most susceptible to parasites and related ailments. This confirmed the

central conclusion of Hamilton and Zuk's theory. Upon surveying studies of the blood-parasite levels of birds from Europe and North America, Read found a clear correlation: the species with the greatest numbers of parasites were indeed those with the most brightly coloured males. These differences between species provide strong support for the idea that mate choice favours individuals which can advertise their health, where health is an issue. Species in which disease is not an issue in mate selection will be correspondingly more drab.

The actual effect of blood parasites on the reproductive success of wild birds is not well known. But a study of kestrels revealed that as many as half of the breeding kestrels have malarial parasites and that the greater the degree of infection, the lower the pair's reproductive success. This situation in itself

Ever alert for the slightest movement of potential prey, a kestrel surveys its surroundings from a tree-branch perch (far left). Displaying muted yet elegant tones, the male and female kestrel differ slightly in colour: the male, which provides most of the food for the young, is chestnut and grey; the female, which incubates and tends the offspring, is reddish brown with black streaks. The pigmentation patterns of birds such as the black-capped chickadee (above) may signal information about the identity, age and social status of an individual.

37

provides the female with an adaptive reason for choosing a healthy-looking male. In populations where parasitism is less of an issue, females will gain less from scrutinizing male health, and correspondingly, males will not be selected to evolve such conspicuous advertisements.

Female birds can also profit from being beautiful. Both sexes of the territorial and monogamous spotted calf bird, another bowerbird, have beautiful emerald-green plumage and bright red eyes. Beauty, then, need not be a consequence only of sexual selection but can result from social selection as well. Competition between females may lead to the development of beautiful plumage in the same way that male rivalry has led to beautiful and ornate males. Recognizing this possibility made me take a new look at common visitors to our bird feeder.

Various woodpeckers, nuthatches and chickadees seem to be exceptions to the generalization that males tend to be more beautiful than females, for the females of these species are often as boldly patterned as the males.

Evolutionary biologist Mary Jane West-Eberhard points out that this is probably the result of social selection—advertising territorial status through colours that demonstrate sexual maturity and health. Most brightly coloured female birds are found in species that are year-round residents and have a monogamous mating system in which both the male and female defend a territory against other members of their own sex. Developing bright and beautiful plumage to indicate competitive status is useful to territorial females. This is also true for male and female toucans and most par-

An emerald toucanet (above) uses its long bill for feeding, plucking fruit from branches or nestlings from deep tree cavities. But the colour of the bill is related to its use in courtship displays. Male and female Australian rainbow lorikeets (right) are equally brilliant, a characteristic of most parrots. Parrots are a family in which monogamy, cavity nesting and defence of the tree hole by a male/female pair against other pairs are common.

while in the Tropics, it is colourful and easily distinguishable. My guess is that temperate-zone female tanagers are not typically engaged in female dominance contests and territorial conflicts. They do not defend a territory when they migrate and are not overtly territorial during the summer. By contrast, tropical female tanagers either defend a territory year-round or fight for status when they join foraging flocks.

Avian ecologist Raleigh Robertson of Queen's University at Kingston, Ontario, and Bridget Stutchbury of Yale University have documented the same phenomenon in tree swallows. Competition among females for nest boxes is apparently intense, with females pecking one another's skulls bare, damaging eyes and even killing each other. Not all female tree swallows are equally beautiful. Only the mature, highly competitive females develop the swallow's trademark shimmering purple, blue-black colouring, while yearling females that are poor competitors wear brown plumage. In this species, at least, beauty is a signal of competitive status.

Nonevolutionary Romantics

How do these theories and studies affect bird watchers? My own experience is that birds seem to grow more beautiful as I become more capable of discerning the meaning of their appearance and behaviour. The iridescent female tree swallow shines not just with light but with accomplishment. Nevertheless, some naturalists remain hostile to the Darwinian interpretation of nature. Part of their reaction is due to the mistaken notion that science is mere number crunching. Naturalist Charlton Ogburn, for instance, has written much on bird behaviour. He argues that "science can tell us nothing about beauty because beauty is something science cannot begin to identify with, let alone measure."

Those who are not biologists often imagine that there is an antipathy between aesthetic experience and explanation. While Keats warned that philosophy would "unweave a rainbow," it is actually evolutionary science that allows us to appreciate

The courtship ceremonies of monogamous seabirds such as the black-browed albatrosses (above) are based on joint male/female rituals like mutual preening, rather than on displays of male brilliance. The vivid patches of bare facial skin displayed by the king vulture (far right) may advertise the health of the bird; blood parasites and other avian illnesses can often be detected by discoloration of the combs, wattles and bare skin.

rots—both sexes defend their nest holes; male and female seabirds also share the defence of their nesting territories. Since most seabirds are monogamous for life, sexual selection for mate-attraction ability is an unlikely architect of their bold-coloured plumage. Instead, the bright colour patterns are probably social signals directed against territorial rivals.

Just as sexual selection may account for patterns in male beauty, so may social selection explain the range of female conspicuousness. For example, differences in the degree of female territoriality might be the reason the coloration of female tanagers in the temperate zone is greenish and dull,

Thoreau's romantic and spiritual hopes for nature. He was referring to scarlet tanagers when he wrote: "We soon get through with Nature. She excites an expectation she cannot satisfy . . . . The red-bird which is the last of Nature is but the first of God . . . . That forest on whose skirts the red-bird flits is not of earth. I expected a fauna more infinite and various, birds of more dazzling colours and more celestial song."

The brilliance of the tanager was mere wild sensation with no larger meaning to Thoreau. Although Darwin did not write quite as poetically, he saw more meaning in the beauty of birds like tanagers. In their feathers, he saw the drive to reproduce struggling against predation—life pitted against death. There is no theme more profound for any living creature. In this sense, Darwin contains Thoreau, and it is something of a tragedy that millions of naturalists continue to read Thoreau while ignoring Darwin.

It is true that the Darwinian view reduces beauty to a biological adaptation. As a result of such reductionism, many naturalists feel, as Harvard University sociobiologist E. O. Wilson puts it, that "scientists are conquistadors who smelt down the Inca gold." But does scientific reductionism kill spiritual beauty for the bird watcher and thereby extinguish the fire of the tanager? I have argued otherwise.

In an essay entitled "The White Bird," art critic John Berger explains the impression of intense beauty as the result of an interaction that affirms something in the viewer. In Berger's words, "What is and what we can see (and by seeing also feel) sometimes meet at a point of affirmation. This point, this coincidence, is two-faced: what has been seen is recognized and affirmed, and at the same time, the seer is affirmed by what he sees . . . . The aesthetic emotion before nature derives, I believe, from this double affirmation."

The beauty of Darwinian nature is to be found in the recognition of that double affirmation. Down by the stream where water and time flow by, the fire of the tanager burns, before us and within us.

the unity of form and content in nature. The aversion of nonscientists to the style of science is understandable. Scientific books and journals focus on facts and hypotheses, rather than on emotion and insight. Ploughing through their arid jargon is too much like work, which is why Thoreau makes for livelier reading than does Darwin. But Darwin saw more deeply into the meaning of nature, and his vision takes us further than the nonevolutionary romantics.

Thoreau, for example, wrote several times about the male scarlet tanager, which he recognized as "our highest-coloured bird . . . . You can hardly believe that a living creature can wear such colours." For Thoreau, the scarlet tanager was a bird that "embraces the wildness and wealth of the woods." But the bird was not enough for

SONG

Interpreting the nature of music

The male house wren (left) returns to reclaim its previous year's territory well ahead of the female. Its complex ascending and descending song is initially a territorial warning to other males; but when the females make their appearance, the male augments its song with high-pitched elements that assist it in its courtship rites.

A hermit thrush helped me leave the only real job I ever had. Resigning from a position at a large American university was difficult in 1980. All the evidence called into question the wisdom of the move: I had no other income to fall back on; my colleagues held that voluntarily jumping off the tenure track was a sure sign of insanity, an argument buttressed by the fact that there were more than 200 eager applicants for the vacancy; friends and relatives pronounced my proposed career in nature writing a blueprint for penury. But a summer spent in the Colorado Rockies being counselled by the music of the hermit thrush made the decision an easy one.

The hermit's song is among the most beautiful in North America. It begins with a low, extended tone that flows out pure and liquid and then dances up flutelike and twists into a delicate phrase. After a pause, it begins again, sometimes with a variation in pitch but always following the same pattern, a pentatonic scale like that used in much of our most ancient human music.

The song poured out of the spruce groves that summer as I hiked below the snowcaps. The silvery phrase matched the clarity of the mountain air and light, and it embodied the peacefulness of life above the clamouring, clawing hubbub of academia. Its lyric argued the rightness of spending more time enjoying nature and less time as a member of the Committee on Committees. The song itself, of course, was no Pied Piper's lure. It was simply a sonorous embodiment of my emotional state.

My emotional response to the music of the hermit thrush, although highly subjective, was not unique. Nor was it arbitrary. In the same way that the song of the nightingale affected European poets such as Keats, the hermit thrush has moved New World writers and poets. Significantly, there is a consistency in the sort of emotions evoked in different listeners when they have heard its song. For example, Thoreau said the bird was "right about the slavery question." For him, its song was an eloquent statement about freedom. Something in the hermit's

43

tune harmonizes with the deeper chords of human emotion and gives them an audible form. Walt Whitman heard the hermit voice his own mourning for Abraham Lincoln:

From the deep secluded recesses,
From the fragrant cedars and the ghostly
*   pines so still,*
Came the carol of the bird.

And the charm of the carol rapt me,
As I held as if by their hands my comrades
*   in the night,*
And the voice of my spirit tallied the song
*   of the bird.*

The curious naturalist must wonder why some birds are emotive musical singers and others jar the ear with their cries. Is there a reason the thrush is so smoothly eloquent while some birds, like the rooster, survive and prosper with a raucous yell?

The answers found in biology books sometimes fail to mention the significance of a bird song's emotional and aesthetic impact and thereby overlook its primary effect on the listener. *Biological Science*, a book used in my freshman biology course and one that is still a best-seller in the field, claims: "Objective investigation has demonstrated that bird song functions primarily as a species-recognition signal." The author, the late William Keeton of Cornell University, cites evidence showing that wood thrushes and their relatives cannot recognize each other by sight alone. The wood thrush will pummel a model of a male Swainson's thrush even when there is no genetic rivalry. But if thrushes hear each other's distinctive songs, they react peaceably.

For a long while, some biologists believed that species recognition for courtship and territoriality was the beginning and end of bird-song biology, which has important implications for understanding the significance of the way different birds sing. If distinctiveness is a song's sole function, then courtship signals, like bird song, might be arbitrary in design. To prevent attraction of the wrong species and to avoid hybridization, it is only essential that the signal be

distinctive enough to attract a mate of the appropriate species. How each species achieves its uniqueness through the use of different melodies, tones and rhythms is of no particular importance, and if this is why bird species sing different songs, emotional reaction to bird songs might be just anthropomorphic baggage of no scientific value.

It is not surprising that many naturalists have chafed at the difference between their emotional response to a bird's song and the cut-and-dried notion that the song says "I am a loon" or "This is my territory." Author Louis Halle complained that "the territorial theory . . . tells me why the nightingale sings. . . . It does not tell me why the night-

ingale sings beautifully." Naturalist/writer Annie Dillard echoes this in her response to mockingbirds: "If the lyric is simply 'mine, mine, mine,' then why the extravagance of the score?" And naturalist Charlton Ogburn asked of the wood thrush that plays "the first three notes of an E-minor chord, next the three of a C natural, then proceeds through a variety of harmonic structures, sometimes sounding a vibrato on a tiny cymbal, to achieve—for us—heart-melting effects. . . . Why have we this rhapsody?" The theory of bird song as simply a matter of recognition is mute on such questions.

The species-recognition idea does not preclude the possibility that other selective

forces have shaped the sound of avian music, however. For example, birds may make aesthetic choices about bird song that are influenced by their habitat or life history. Christopher Loffredo and Gerald Borgia of the University of Maryland have found that certain forms of song are associated with particular kinds of mating systems. They compared related species with polygynous and monogamous mating systems. Using recordings, Loffredo and Borgia analyzed the songs of 158 species in nine bird families, including cotingas, pheasants, manakins, weavers, parrots, bowerbirds, birds of paradise, bulbuls and sandpipers. In these families, some species

are characteristically monogamous, while others are polygynous, with some males mating with many females.

Loffredo and Borgia argued that in polygynous species, where the male offers no material contribution whatsoever to the female—no parental care, no territory, no feeding resource—the only chance a female has to better herself evolutionarily is to choose a high-quality male. A small number of males often gain the majority of copulations as a result of their ability to court effectively and to defeat or intimidate other males. Loffredo and Borgia predicted that the male's song conveys information about his size, age, health and social status.

There is nothing musical about the harsh call of the bald eagle (above) or about that of most of its raptor relatives. Both sexes use their limited set of noises to communicate with one another. The male yellow-headed blackbird (left) sings almost continuously during the daylight hours of its breeding season. Its song acts as a deterrent to rival males, and males that are unable to sing suffer a greater rate of territorial intrusions.

Birds such as the Manchurian crane (above) often call with a high-decibel and variable-frequency honk. Since smaller and weaker birds are unable to create such a call, the bird that produces a loud and deeply pitched sound is reliably signalling its size and vigour to mates and rivals. Like many corvids, these Clark's nutcrackers (far right) have a large vocal repertoire. Sometimes, they communicate with rhythmic clacking and churring noises; at other times, they produce melodious music. The significance of different bird vocalizations is often difficult to determine.

By contrast, monogamous male birds usually provide some form of parental care or defend a territory or nesting site of value to the female. In such a system, the male's song might be designed to convey other useful information, such as presence, proximity and individual identity. It is essential that a female be able to assess the presence of her mate when the two are coordinating incubation, feeding and territorial defence.

Loffredo and Borgia therefore predicted that there would be differences between the songs of monogamous and polygynous birds as a result of differences in their choice of mating system. Polygynous systems, they reasoned, should favour qualities unlike those useful in monogamous situations. The alternative prediction was that if song characteristics are, in fact, arbitrary and are used only for species recognition, then no

pattern of differences should exist between the monogamous and the polygynous birds.

In order to study bird vocalizations, Loffredo and Borgia played the songs into a digital sound analyzer, which made it possible to calculate the frequency range. In addition, the calls were classified according to whether they consisted of whistles and other relatively pure tones or of noisy slurring, buzzing, booming and clicking sounds with variable frequencies. When the results were tallied, clear differences emerged between the two mating systems. Males of the polygynous species had relatively noisy variable-frequency songs. They used a greater range of frequencies, with many more buzzes, clicks, booms and slurs than monogamous species. The monogamous species were more musical and relied on whistles and phrases of relatively pure tones. According to Loffredo and Borgia, the noisy and variable vocalizations of polygynous males are aggressive signals related to dominance interactions at mating sites. Males within a species differ in their ability to create aggressive vocal displays, and the individual differences provide females with cues for choosing a high-status mate.

Eugene Morton of the Smithsonian Institution argues that such a difference is no arbitrary accident. The physics of sound production, Morton points out, implies that producing loud low-pitched sounds requires a larger vocal apparatus than does producing weaker sounds of higher pitch. Since size usually determines fighting success, a bird ought to avoid combat with an individual able to generate lower-pitched noises than it can produce itself. Selection will then favour aggressive displays that feature noisy low-pitched sounds.

Morton's theory confirms common human experience and perception. We recognize the low growl of a dog as a sign of aggression, while a high whimpering indicates appeasement and submission. So, too, without our ever seeing a rooster or a turkey, we can tell from their songs alone that the crowing rooster and the gobbling tom are big, pugilistic, polygynous birds. There is some congruence between our reaction to bird song and its meaning in avian nature.

Listening to Nature

For naturalists, this is a satisfying finding. Since so many unrelated species converged on the same noisy pattern of vocalization, it would appear that courtship song is far from an arbitrary signal. Instead, the particular way some birds sound reflects adaptive design. Trying to discover design in the sound of a bird is one of the pleasures of listening to nature. The fact that recognizable patterns can be demonstrated confirms this pleasure.

We can use adaptive thinking to understand our own interpretations of the songs we hear. Not long ago, I listened to a bird perform a rhapsody new to my ears. I was lying under a mosquito net in a shack in the Peñas Blancas Valley of Costa Rica. It was

five in the morning, still dark in the forest, and someone said, "Listen to his call." I could hear a long, deep monotone, as though someone were blowing across the top of an empty bottle. Again and again, the note droned out of the foggy canopy. It was the call of the bare-necked umbrella bird, one of the rare and little-known cotingids.

The bottle-blowing simile is a useful one. In Peñas Blancas, long, rainy nights are often brightened by candlelight conversation and a bottle of cheap rum passed from hand to hand. At such times, someone inevitably blows across the bottle mouth from time to time. As the bottle gets emptier, the pitch of the sound becomes lower and lower. When it is completely empty, one can create not only a close imitation of the mature male umbrella bird's song but perhaps a credible explanation of why song

47

The male sedge, or short-billed marsh, wren (right) sings a simple song compared with those of many other wrens. The limited size of its repertoire suggests that song plays less of a role in courtship than it does in other species, such as the marsh wren (above), whose large song repertoire varies from one population to another. In monogamous populations, repertoires are relatively small; in polygynous populations where a male mates with several females, song repertoires may be large and include hundreds of different songs.

can be a helpful size-assessment device.

The larger and emptier the bottle, the lower the note. Similarly, the bigger the bird, the lower and perhaps the longer the note it will produce. If this is true, then a low-note performance contains information about male size and maturity. Indeed, one of my friends informs me that young male umbrella birds seem unable to produce the deep throaty tones.

Being aware of the information in a bird's song helps us find new significance in commonplace phenomena. I have always taken it for granted that birds sing most effusively at dawn. But Bruce Lyon and Bob Montgomerie, two behavioural ecologists who study birds, point out that this exuberant dawn chorus is in fact a great enigma, a mystery I have listened to every morning of my life and failed to comprehend.

Most of the songbirds that join in the dawn chorus have high metabolisms. During the long night, they burn energy at a great rate, often losing 5 percent of their body weight between dusk and dawn. It makes sense that the first thing a bird would do upon waking would be to forage; instead, the males sing loudly and vigorously in a performance that must burn even more energy. Some biologists have suggested that the reason an intense bout of song takes place at dawn is that air turbulence is lower and song is more effectively carried. Others have argued that dim-light foraging is inefficient or that the risk of attracting predators is lower at this time. For their part, Lyon and Montgomerie suggest that only males in good condition can afford to sing at dawn and are, in effect, advertising their quality. None of these ideas have been rigorously

monogamous. The western male repertoire, containing as many as 210 songs, averages three times the diversity of the eastern male's repertoire. The western males also devote 50 percent more brain area to vocalization than do eastern males. This fits with what we know about polygynous mating systems, which favour males with the most developed courtship and territorial displays. The males that mate with the most females sire the most offspring. By contrast, where monogamy is common, such as in the eastern United States, males that are best able to rear offspring are favoured. A diverse repertoire is less useful under these conditions, and the valuable brain space that could be devoted to a large repertoire would be better employed in other tasks, such as finding food.

Is it possible that female birds actually find one male's vocal performance more beautiful than another's and are emotionally influenced by a bravura singing performance? Females that experience pleasure when a good performance is heard and respond by mating with the singer will be favoured by natural selection. As long as the link exists, selection can operate on aesthetic responses and designs, just as it can mould a wing or colour a feather.

Charles Hartshorne, author of a detailed interpretation of bird song, has pursued some of the semantic issues raised by Darwin's suggestion that birds do react aesthetically to displays such as song. According to Hartshorne, some people fail to recognize that not all aesthetic reactions require the self-conscious introspection we are capable of as a result of our large human brains. He argues, validly in my opinion, that there is a difference between aesthetic feeling and aesthetic thought. An aesthetic reaction is something that varies both in intensity and in the type of response evoked — pleasure, boredom, disgust or fear — as a result of a stimulus. The difference between bird and human responses to a stimulus is qualitative, not absolute.

It may be a long time before we can look deeper into a bird's emotional state. But we can at least observe birds and determine

tested, but they do serve to illustrate the fact that biologists now hear far more than merely mate recognition in the sounds of birds at daybreak.

Repertoire Variation

One of the remarkable features of bird song is the radical variation in repertoires. While the umbrella bird uses only one note, species such as the mockingbird sing as many as 412 different songs in succession. Ovenbirds, some sparrows, buntings and flycatchers get by with one or two types of song; song sparrows use as many as 10 different songs; various wrens sing several dozen to a few hundred songs; and brown thrashers learn more than 2,000 songs. It is difficult to explain the differences among species. We can explore the question of repertoire variation, though, by asking

whether repertoire size has any effect on an individual's reproductive success.

Some birds are born knowing their song: the eastern phoebe's simple song is genetically inherited and instinctive. The large repertoires of many songbirds, however, are learned. Mockingbirds learn new types of song each year, and so do male redwings and starlings. In general, it is the older males in a population that have the largest repertoires, which suggests that song diversity is some measure of a male's ability to survive and learn.

Donald Kroodsma of the University of Massachusetts has found that repertoire richness of marsh wrens correlates with the mating system found in different populations. In San Francisco area marshes, males tend to be polygynous, while in eastern U.S. populations, marsh wrens are more often

Territorial displays are evolutionarily designed to be impressive to rivals and mates. The loud "conka-reé" call of the male red-winged blackbird (left) is given as it spreads its wings to enhance its body size and flashes its bright wing badges to indicate its age and experience. Song has a certain advantage over plumage coloration as a courtship and territorial signal. The camouflaged swamp sparrow (above) can become muted and hard to locate when threatened by a predator; brightly coloured birds are unable to conceal themselves.

whether they respond selectively to songs of different quality. In the field, it is often hard to tell whether females are attracted by a male's territorial quality or by his displays. The two are often positively correlated. However, there is now experimental evidence that female birds are attracted to and stimulated by enlarged repertoires. Female canaries are more inclined to build nests when they hear large repertoires than when they hear smaller ones. Captive redwing females court more vigorously in response to a recording of multiple song types than they do to a broadcast of just one song. Swamp and song sparrow females will also court more readily when they hear multiple song types.

It may not be the repertoire alone that attracts females, since in many species, such as red-winged blackbirds, the males with

enlarged repertoires also have high-quality territories. In fact, this is what we expect. Repertoire size is merely one more attribute signalling male quality. Presumably, it is when females and males both begin to rely heavily on this trait as a measure of a male's value as a mate that the repertoire proliferates as a result of sexual selection.

Sexual selection, however, is not responsible for the more intricate avian songs. The most complicated bird songs are the duets that monogamous pairs sing together. The most amazing duets are those sung by wrens and shrikes. They countersing rapidly, with each bird supplying a few of the notes in an extended phrase. In the tangled deciduous forest of northwestern Costa Rica, I have listened to rufous-naped wrens dueting so smoothly that it is hard to believe there are two birds chiming in and out. They sing with

staccato doublets, shifting pitch, slurring, whistling and chattering, in cadences they can repeat again and again. In order to appreciate the coordination of the duet, we must really see them perform it. What seems to be one bird singing turns out to be two in perfect synchrony.

Duets occur among some northern birds as well. Cardinals duet extensively, as do drumming downy and hairy woodpeckers. The mournful wail of loons echoing down a northern lake is often a reciprocal contact call between a mated pair. But duets are most common in dense tropical forest. The extensive development of dueting in tropical forest is thought to be a means of maintaining contact and establishing the position of one's mate in heavy vegetation, where visual clues are limited, and it occurs where the male and female share a permanent territory. Pairs will duet in response to the sound of neighbours and to each other. In other words, the duet serves the same territorial and mate-guarding functions as do most bird songs.

Many duets are punctuated with whistles and other syllables of clear tonal sounds. Studies of the song of the white-throated

sparrow suggest that the pure tones in the song facilitate individual recognition. There also seems to be a physical reason for the flutelike tones of dueting forest birds. The pure-tone sounds are more effective in penetrating dense vegetation than are variable-tone sounds, which tend to be absorbed and degraded more quickly.

Eugene Morton established the connection between pure tones and the density of vegetation by analyzing the relationship between song structure and habitat for 177 different Neotropical birds occupying forest, edge and grassland habitats. He made recordings of the songs and rebroadcast them with loudspeakers in the different habitats; then, by rerecording them at different distances, he was able to measure the way in which different song types degraded as they passed through the vegetation.

It is necessary to recall that sound travels in waves whose length is inversely related to frequency: the higher the frequency, the shorter the wavelength. Differences in the size of the waves determine how readily they are absorbed or pass by an obstacle. In general, short, high-frequency waves should be absorbed more easily. Long

waves pass around objects and typically travel farther. That is why the low hoot of an owl travels a greater distance than the high-pitched squeak of its mouse victim, even though both calls are given with the same intensity.

Morton, however, discovered that the relationship was modified by the structure of the habitat. In the forest, an intermediate frequency travelled farther than a lower or higher one. The structure of the forest seemed to create a sound window in which tones of 1.5 to 2.5 kHz frequency travelled efficiently. Many forest birds broadcast relatively pure tonal songs within this frequency range, thereby increasing their ability to reach their audiences. Conversely, the sound window and the flutelike whistling tendency was absent in the grassland birds. Open-habitat birds tended to use buzzy calls that swept through a wide range of frequencies.

Morton argued that this strategy is an adaptation to the turbulent atmosphere of the open, often windy habitat. Using a song based on a changing pattern of sound means that individual recognition and communication is still possible even if some frequencies are absorbed by turbulence. When he compared closely related vireos and antbirds living in the two habitats, he found that open and edge species used variable-frequency songs and forest species relied more on pure, flutelike songs. Morton's ambitious study shows that the acoustic environment can cause selection for certain song designs, just as sexual selection or social signalling can.

Naturalists have long been aware of these connections. More than half a century ago, the great bird artist Louis Agassiz Fuertes wrote a series about the voices of tropical birds. When he spoke of the open, brushy pastures of the Andes, he mentioned "the shrill piping . . . the insistent kekking . . . the dry, phoebe-like fret . . . and the lisping insect songs" of the habitat's characteristic birds. As he moved to the forest, he mentioned the "leisurely whistling . . . velvet smoothness . . . silver note . . . violin tones" of the forest birds. Morton has brought to light the design principles that explain Fuertes' impressions.

Beauty of Form

I am still unable to catch the nuances Morton or Fuertes might detect in a song. But even to me, there seems to be a congruence in the sounds of dense-forest birds. In Central American or Andean cloud forest, I am always struck by the shining metallic phrase of the solitaires. They arouse much the same emotions that hermit or wood thrushes do. Just as the hermit thrush's song expressed the wildness of the eastern mixed deciduous forest for Thoreau, the silvery whistle of a solitaire evokes the loneliness of the Andean cloud forest.

The convergence and emotional association of a flutelike song with wild, dense forest raises a persistent question for the naturalist: How much of what moves us actually corresponds to something ecologically or behaviourally significant?

Darwin stressed the possible kinship of our emotional reaction to music with that of birds to their music. He pointed out that "we can concentrate . . . greater intensity of feeling in a single musical note than in pages of writing. It is probable that nearly the same emotions, but much weaker and far less complex, are felt by birds when the male pours forth his full volume of song, in rivalry with other males, to captivate the female. Love is still the commonest theme of our songs." Hartshorne agreed that higher types of organisms can have some sympathy and understanding for lower types. Were this not so, he argued, "there would be no science of behaviour."

There is no reason to expect that human responses correspond exactly to those of birds. Nevertheless, it is clear that our aesthetic responses to bird song are reactions to sound patterns which have adaptive significance in nature.

We can further our appreciation of avian music simply by becoming more aware of the form that exists in what we hear. In *The Musical Companion*, musicologist Roger North notes: "We always speak of music as if it were the sounds themselves; in fact, it is the experience of them." According to North, "Great music is great because of its beauty of form and because of the emotions engendered by listening to it, which are largely a function of the beauty of form." For the naturalist, the enjoyment of bird song is derived from both the experience of the music and the recognition of its forms and their meaning.

Consider Thoreau again. We can only speculate about why he was so moved by the hermit thrush's song. Perhaps it was because its song has a complex structure that recalls much of our own music. Perhaps it was because whenever Thoreau heard the song, he was alone in a forest that seemed wild and free, and ever after, he associated the song with wilderness and freedom. He wrote about the hermit thrush precisely because he had made that connection. I expect Thoreau would have enjoyed exploring that congruence further and recognizing the adaptive link between the hermit's pure tonal melody and its wild, thick-forest habitat. And I have no doubt he would have welcomed the idea that birds possess an emotional response to the sound of their own music.

Duets are commonly sung by monogamously paired birds that live in areas of thick vegetation where visual contact is difficult or by birds such as loons (far left) that forage far apart and nocturnally. Male/female duets are among the most intricate of all bird songs, and they may function as a mate-guarding mechanism. The meadowlark (above) has several different song types in its repertoire and may shift from one type to another several times during the day. When a male changes its song, an adjacent male might also alter its song type to match its rival's. By shifting songs, a meadowlark may be testing the alertness of a rival; by matching the new song, the rival proves its readiness.

MATING

Reproductive success and the rites of spring

Standing erect on its drumming log, a territorial male ruffed grouse (left) beats its wings to produce a deep thudding sound. The display, repeated every few minutes during breeding season, begins slowly, quickly accelerating into a crescendo of sound as the flailing wings blur with speed. The drumming, which can be heard for half a mile, is a powerful signal that attracts widely dispersed females and repels male rivals.

As spring approaches and the days brighten, the wooded hills around our house begin thudding with the sound of courting grouse. The territorial male ruffed grouse advertises its presence with a loud wing-drumming display. Its drumming site is often the trunk of an old fallen tree whose green mossy coat is worn bare by the bird's tread. The grouse stands erect on the trunk and spreads its wings, flapping them downward suddenly. The cupping and compressing of the air under them produces a booming wave of sound. As the drumming builds into a crescendo, the grouse's wings blur with speed. The force of its flapping completely occupies the grouse, and in spite of snapping twigs and crackling leaves, a person can come close enough to watch the performance.

Sometimes, the drummer walks back and forth along the trunk, scanning the understorey, perhaps looking for the approach of a female grouse, perhaps watching for a fox. If it detects something out of place or discerns your presence, immobile and half-hidden by a tree trunk though you are, the male steps down and, with high, slow steps, stealthily moves away. With its mottled, russet plumage, it is virtually invisible, part of the carpet of weathered oak and maple leaves. Only when it is suddenly startled will the grouse explode into a wild weaving flight through the forest.

How different are the courtship ritual and character of the ruffed grouse from those of the spruce grouse in the coniferous forest just to the north—a bird whose complete lack of stealth and caution has always mystified me. I have often encountered the large, plump spruce grouse sitting at eye level on a spruce limb right beside a trail, seemingly oblivious to me. The consequence of its monotonous diet of conifer needles, with their terpenes and essential oils, is an unsavoury flavour of turpentine in its meat—a protection that makes fear of large mammals unnecessary for this grouse.

The fearlessness of the spruce grouse is not the only difference between the "fool hens" and the related ruffed grouse; their

55

courtship displays are also very dissimilar. In the midst of the boreal fastness, where miles of spring-green forest lie quiet and still, mantled in the ebbing snows of winter, the peace is broken by what sounds like a large, demented owl. The male spruce grouse hoots, shakes and wheezes, apparently ridiculously intoxicated when under the influence of mating hormones. It lurches across clearings in short, noisy flights of rattling wing feathers that sound like a helicopter passing overhead. No one could ever confuse these tame and laughable birds with the nervous and stealthy ruffed grouse.

The mating rites of the sage and sharptailed grouse of the open western grasslands, sage plains and bushy rangeland differ tremendously from those of grouse species in either woodland or arctic-alpine habitats. Instead of being dispersed, sage grouse males congregate at traditional display sites known as leks. Usually, the lek is located on a prominence—a rounded hill or open arena-like area that is highly visible. Literally hundreds of males show up at these sites year after year to perform their mating displays. There is great competition—kicking, bumping and pecking—for control of a small territory of a few square yards in the central part of the lek.

Male sage grouse are much larger and more ornate than the females and have massive esophageal chest sacs highlighted in white plumage that hold more than five litres of air. The male's throat sac is used in a coordinated display that involves several complicated elements. The yellow combs over the eyes thicken, the throat and head feathers become erect, and the wings are drawn back against special feathers along the body that produce a swishing sound. The throat sac expands and contracts; the mass of air in the sac resonates with a cooing noise and then swells two bare, yellow skin pockets in the neck that give off popping noises. The females inspect the males as they go through their elaborate routine of strutting, swishing, cooing and popping, and the hens show a definite preference for centrally located males. These males obtain most of the females, which copulate once and then disperse over a great area.

Each grouse species has a distinctive set of courtship behaviours. In fact, every one of the more than 8,600 bird species has a unique song or dance or other mating ritual. Learning the details of each species' display is one of the fascinating aspects of bird study. But the incredible diversity of behaviour is confusing without a system of

56

ideas and names by which to organize it. Classification of mating behaviour helps the naturalist see and understand the connections between a bird's habitat, its food and the way it mates and reproduces.

When biologists compared different grouse mating behaviours, they found a clear link between habitat and behaviour. Lekking grouse seem to live in open, arid habitats, while the grouse with dispersed territorial males, such as ruffed grouse, live in woodland habitats. The former's exposure to predators is one possible explanation for the evolution of leks — a large group has many eyes to spot an approaching hawk or coyote. For the latter group, however, the low visibility in spruce or deciduous woodland means that lekking might actually increase predation risk. Predation on ruffed grouse, for example, is higher at drumming sites used year after year than at first-time drumming sites, which suggests that predators can home in on drummers in woodland habitats.

Avian Mating Systems

Habitat identification helps us see patterns in the diversity of mating behaviour, but more fundamental criteria are needed to give us an understanding of the system of avian mating. First, biologists consider a crucial item: the number of mates a male or female has during a breeding season. Monogamy means having one mate during the breeding season; polygyny refers to a male's mating with more than one female; and polyandry describes the mating of a female with more than one male. The label "promiscuous" is used when both sexes have multiple partners. The system can then be fine-tuned by considering what ecological and evolutionary forces influence the number of mates a male or female obtains.

The predominant mating system of birds is a monogamous pairing, in which the male contributes to nest building, defence, incubation and feeding. This version of monogamy is typical of birds that hunt either large prey or prey that are erratically distributed over a great area. Monogamous seabirds such as albatrosses, shearwaters

and frigate birds often travel hundreds of miles on each foraging circuit.

Frigate birds bear witness to the range of their voyages both in their reproductive biology and in their appearance. With huge wings and forked tails, they look like giant kites and are highly adapted for soaring and sailing, having feathers that actually weigh more than their skeletons. Their feet and legs are reduced, and they rarely land except at their nesting and roosting sites. They spend long hours aloft, searching for unusual and widely scattered prey items. I have watched frigate birds arrive at the hatch of young ridley sea turtles at dawn. As the hatchling turtles make their way seaward, the frigates glide gracefully along, inches above the sand and surf, and skilfully pluck up the waddling and bobbing turtles with their long, hooked bills.

On range and grassland, sage grouse congregate in courtship and mating arenas known as leks (far left). The huge male displays its elaborate fan of tail feathers and inflates its massive throat sacs as it stamps and puffs in a vigorous performance for its audience of females. The smaller, well-camouflaged females choose males according to their position in the mating arena and to the strength of certain features in their display. After mating, the male and female grouse have no further contact, whereas monogamously paired birds, like these black-browed albatrosses found on the Falkland Islands (above), continue to engage in greeting and courtship rituals during the long breeding and nesting period. The male has assumed a ritualized posture as it approaches its mate.

biparental care requirement varies greatly both among and within species. With tree swallows nesting in Ontario, the male does roughly half the feeding of the nestlings. If a mate is removed, the fledgling success rate generally drops substantially, which means that a male must remain to help if the offspring are to survive. The value of male parental care, however, is related to food availability. In Alberta, where insect swarms are more abundant, or in highly productive areas near sewage ponds and marshes, females are able to rear clutches without male assistance. Similarly, food gathering is a flexible contribution for male bobolinks: under good foraging conditions, when the weather is favourable and insects are plentiful, the male bobolink supplies 40 percent of the food for nestlings; but if the foraging conditions are poor, the male boosts its contribution by supplying 60 percent of their food requirement.

Often, a demand for something other than food gathering most directly influences parental care. Predation on the nestlings and competition for nest sites both make biparental care essential. In bird colonies where there is intense competition for nest sites, an adult must remain resident to fend off the constant intrusions of interlopers. Storks and herons without a nest site will evict undefended nestlings in an attempt to take over the nest. In addition, gulls, ravens and other predators are attracted to bird colonies as a ready food source, and they quickly haul undefended offspring away.

To determine which ecological forces actually favour monogamy in a particular species, Kathy Martin of Queen's University at Kingston, Ontario, explored more fully the system of male and female monogamy in willow ptarmigan. She sought to assess whether a male remained with its mate to reduce predation on its mate and nestlings or to guard against cuckoldry.

Martin worked in the open sub-Arctic tundra near Churchill, Manitoba, an area of willow shrub. To find birds, she used English setters trained as ptarmigan spotters. The birds were either noosed or netted and then colour-banded to make

I have also seen frigates skimming over the water like a vanguard at the leading edge of a tuna pack on the rampage. As the tuna school races along just below the surface, a bow wave of panicking bait fish marks its approach. The small, silvery fish leap wriggling into the air in an effort to escape the tuna. But a frigate bird is often there in anticipation, ahead of the tuna, snagging the fish as they leap for safety. Neither turtle hatches nor tuna schools are predictable occurrences, and frigates must spend much of their time in flight searching for adequate food. This makes monogamy a necessity: one bird must spend long hours foraging, and the other must defend the nest. Both sexes of a pair of frigates take turns incubating their single egg.

Sit-and-Wait Predators

The same food-related constraint orchestrates the reproduction of raptors that are specialized for feeding on large prey. They spend long periods of time searching or waiting for their prey. Harpy eagles and ornate hawk-eagles, which live in the forests of Central and South America, hunt monkeys and other large arboreal mammals. They are sit-and-wait predators that perch at vantage points in the canopy of the forest

and watch for a troop of unsuspecting monkeys to pass. Monkeys are keen hawk detectors, however. I have watched the smaller, and hence more vulnerable, species of monkeys such as capuchins or squirrel monkeys and been struck by their alert nervousness. They are constantly looking around, scanning the foliage and chattering warnings to each other at the slightest hint of danger. Thus it can take as long as a week for a harpy to capture a prey item. Similarly, other large raptors such as the Andean condor may spend days on the wing, soaring over vast expanses of the Andes in search of a dead llama.

The hunting style of all of these birds, be they albatrosses, frigates or large raptors, appears to require that they be monogamous, with both parents contributing to the rearing of the young, usually only a single offspring per pair; experimental additions of extra eggs or nestlings to the nests of albatrosses, shearwaters and petrels show that a pair of parents cannot gather enough food to rear more than one young at a time — strong evidence that both parents are necessary to feed the offspring.

In songbirds with relatively large clutches and altricial young (born helpless), males often contribute food for nestlings. The

Great horned owls (far left) breed in late winter or early spring, when the weather is still snowy and hunting for rodents and rabbits is good. As with most large raptorial birds, both the male and female incubate the eggs, hunt for food,﹒care for the nestlings and vigorously attack intruders. The great blue heron nestlings perched in their open nest of sticks (above) are vulnerable to predators as well as to other great blue herons. Both parents are needed to defend the nest, since jays and crows eat undefended nestlings, and other herons without nest sites will attempt to take over an undefended nest. While one heron forages, its mate remains at the nest. A male Arctic tern (right) returns with a fish for its newly hatched nestling. Like many monogamous seabirds, arctic terns nest on land yet may forage at sea a considerable distance from the nesting colony. Both the male and female are therefore essential for rearing nestlings.

A gentoo penguin regurgitates a meal of seafood for its two hungry chicks (left). Both parents take turns bringing food in daily, and during incubation, they alternate on egg-warming duty. Choosing a competent mate with good foraging and parental-care ability is crucial to breeding success for this bird. Willow ptarmigan (above), which are found in Arctic habitats, are seen here in their summer plumage. They, too, have a monogamous system in which the male and female share a breeding and foraging territory during the summer months.

identification of each individual possible.

A male willow ptarmigan will vigorously guard its mate and offspring, putting its own life in jeopardy. Male attentiveness reaches a peak during the breeding period in late May and early June. At that time, Martin found that only a tiny proportion of female grouse were sighted alone (233 of 235 females were accompanied by males). By performing experiments designed to assess just what motivated males to attend females so closely, she attempted to determine whether male presence increased the survival rate of their mates. Widowing 27 hens, she compared them with 118 females that retained their mates. All of the widowed birds survived until hatch time, while five of the paired females were killed, indicating that males do not enhance the survival rate of their mates. She also found that widows

maintained their body weight just as well as females with mates, which suggests that in willow ptarmigan, male mate-guarding does not improve the female condition.

In addition, Martin set up an experiment designed to test male priorities when they were given a choice of guarding their mates or defending their offspring. She separated a pair and then observed whether the male guarded its mate or the nest site and offspring. Males were much more likely to guard the female during the preincubation period, the time when copulation with another male could result in fertilization of the eggs. When the female had laid and was incubating, however, the male switched priorities and became more likely to defend the offspring.

Predation was high—80 percent of first clutches in one year and 62 percent in the

The Asian open-bill storks (above) breed when wet-season populations of snails increase. Paired solitary nesting storks usually remain together for several years, while colonially nesting storks tend not to maintain long-term pair-bonds. By contrast, the immense and densely packed gannet colony in Newfoundland (right) is composed of thousands of birds, each of which is monogamously bonded with a partner and possesses a nest site that it recognizes as distinct from all others. Sometimes monogamous in name only, however, males in dense colonies of birds commonly attempt to mate with females other than their own mate.

The risk of cuckoldry by nearby males may explain why a male gannet (above) often copulates more than a hundred times with its mate. The probability that it will be the true genetic father of the nestlings it helps rear is thereby vastly increased. The males of solitary nesting birds, such as these mating red-necked grebes (far right), enjoy a relatively low risk of cuckoldry compared with that experienced by the males of colonial nesters.

next year. Red foxes, ermine, ravens, jaegers and gulls all stole eggs; therefore, there were lots of renesting females and plenty of opportunities for males to refertilize a female. Since not all males obtained a territory, the unpaired males waited, ready to pair with any available females, which explains the inclination of males to stay close to the females during the early part of the breeding period. Male monogamy is best interpreted in this case as a defence against cuckoldry.

Martin's finding is consistent with what is known about monogamy in many waterfowl. Paired birds do better than lone birds in dominance contests and in competition for nest sites. But the continued presence of the male during laying and incubation seems to be male defence against cuckoldry. In snow geese, for example, the male

provides no parental care but remains in close contact with the incubating female. An experiment by Fred Cooke and his associates at Queen's University compared 7 female snow geese without mates with 14 pairs. Among the widows, they recorded five forced copulations, four attacks by males and three chases. An earlier study found that one widow was forced to copulate nine times in the two days following the loss of her mate. By contrast, control females with males were not harassed.

Cuckoldry is the ultimate genetic disaster for the monogamous male bird that makes a large investment in the clutch of one female. The female always propagates her own genes, but a male is never completely assured of his paternity. Genetic analysis has detected a substantial rate of cuckoldry in birds such as indigo buntings, and it is also known to occur in red-winged blackbirds, bobolinks and bluebirds.

Cuckoldry can result either from forced copulations in the absence of the territorial male or when the female actively solicits the extra-pair copulation. Susan Smith of Mount Holyoke College in South Hadley, Massachusetts, has observed female black-capped chickadees soliciting copulations from males other than their mates. In pairs of colour-banded chickadees whose dominance ranks in flocks were known, the female often left the territory shared with its normal mate and moved briefly into the territory of another male and mated with it. In each of the 13 extra-pair copulations, the female mated with a male whose dominance ranking was higher than its normal mate's.

The potential for cuckoldry is especially great for the raptors and seabirds in which pairs are separated by long periods of hunting. Since mate-guarding is not possible, male raptors and seabirds, especially colonial species, often copulate many times with their mates. The goshawk holds the record, copulating up to 600 times with its mate during one breeding season. The gannet, which nests in dense colonies, copulates 100 times in a breeding season. By mating many times, a male at risk of cuckoldry may reduce the probability that another male's sperm will fertilize the eggs of its mate.

In monogamous situations, then, as in all mating systems, the evolutionary interests of the male and female may not coincide. Each has evolved behaviours that maximize its own reproductive success. Females profit by obtaining parental-care assistance from a mate. But by means of extra-pair copulations, a female might genetically diversify her offspring by mating with more than one male. Likewise, a male can gain evolutionarily by cuckolding its neighbour and, in effect, parasitizing a rival's parental care.

The evolutionary conflict of interest between male and female is clearly seen in bird populations in which both monogamy and polygyny are found. Indigo buntings, song sparrows, bobolinks, bluebirds, tree swallows, blackpoll warblers and meadowlarks are a few of the many songbirds whose

essentially monogamous mating systems also include some males that are polygynous. If its territory is particularly rich in either nest sites or food, a male may attract more than one female. Often, the spatial distribution of resources such as nest sites determines the mating system that develops. Orchard orioles, for example, are monogamous when there is plenty of wooded habitat and an abundance of trees

for nest sites. Females under these conditions will not mate with an already paired male. But in open areas with few trees, polygynous groups form, with several females hanging their nests in the tree defended by a territorial male.

The transition from monogamy to polygyny is usually not in the interests of the female. Whatever resources the male may control and whatever parental care it may

provide will be shared among several females. Not surprisingly, then, females in harem-forming species such as redwings oppose, with varying success, the settlement of new females within their territories. Female aggression toward other females can reduce a male's polygynous opportunities.

Polygyny often results when a male is able to monopolize a resource useful to several females. One of the classic examples of such a system is found in red-winged blackbirds. Some males can defend an area of marsh or a productive meadow that will hold the nests of 10 or more females. Nest sites that are both safe from predators and rich in food resources are patchily distributed; thus a male that is successful at excluding other males may have sole sexual access to several females nesting within its defended area. There is also some evidence that redwing polygyny may be based on the variation in quality of parental care provided by males and the attractiveness of that quality to females. Males able to forage effectively may have larger harems.

Redwing mating systems illustrate the problems of definition that accompany any effort at classification. In some areas, a mating system based on resource control might be called "resource-defence polygyny." There is also evidence of "parental-care polygyny" based on the variation in male feeding abilities. And when males defend females that nest together in clumps to avoid predators, the situation is called "harem-defence polygyny." The problem of nomenclature is a consequence of the facts that redwing populations vary in their ecological resources and that male behaviour is not the sole determinant of the mating system. Females choose territories and oppose other females that wish to occupy the same area. A classification system based on the female perspective might use an entirely different set of labels.

Females may settle for being part of a polygynous association when the male can provide an abundance of food. Northern harriers, for example, are usually monogamous, but they switch to polygyny during times of abundance. These birds, also known as marsh hawks, live in open habitats and have distinctive hunting techniques. Harriers are the daytime counterpart of the short-eared owl and specialize in hunting small rodents. I often see them swinging back and forth over the fields in eastern Ontario, in their characteristic flap-and-glide hunting circuit, as they listen for voles.

Their faces are remarkably owl-like, with large, saucer-shaped ruffs of feathers around the ears that enable them to localize the squeak of a rodent with the accuracy of an owl. Although they eat many small animals, harriers seem to be vole specialists. In some years, about every four to six around here, voles grow so numerous that the fields are honeycombed with their runways and dotted with their nests of shredded fibres. The meadows seem to boil with jumping, diving, scurrying voles. Perhaps that is why harriers sometimes lay as many as five eggs, far more than most raptors — to capitalize on the explosion of rodents.

At the peak of the vole outbreak, harriers often become polygynous. Several females may nest in the same marshy meadow, with a single male defending and provisioning the nests. Each time the laden male returns, he calls out to a female. As she leaps into the air and flys up toward him, the male drops the vole for her to catch in flight. The male does this throughout the day, visiting each of the females and doing all of the foraging. Polygyny under such circumstances leaves the females to defend their nests while the shared male forages.

Sexual Dimorphism

Whenever ecological forces result in females clustering their nests and males not providing large amounts of parental care, there is an opportunity for polygyny to evolve. Ornithologist Scott Robinson has made an in-depth study of that mating system by observing yellow-rumped caciques in southeastern Peru. These large blackbirds are among the most conspicuous features of the lowland Amazonian forest. On islands in lakes and rivers and on riverbanks, their woven basketlike nests dangle

A thick-billed murre adult, with head inclined, calls its chick to feed (far left). Although both sexes of this monogamous seabird contribute equal amounts of food to the chick, it is the male that accompanies and defends the fledgling when it finally leaps from its ledge hundreds of feet above the ocean. The common loon agitatedly dancing on the water (above) attempts to divert attention from its mate and nest. Predator-distraction displays represent a costly form of parental investment: they radically increase the probability of death for the parent that performs them. This male-female pair of blue-eyed shags (right) begins the long ritualized courtship that precedes breeding in monogamous seabirds.

Courting birds such as the king penguins (above) engage in exaggerated displays that may appear ludicrous to human observers. Careful examination of courtship rituals, however, has shown that these displays actually signal information about a bird's age, experience and social status. The male prairie chicken (right), which solicits copulation from the standing female by bending over and displaying its spread wings and raised tail, has evolved behaviours designed to maximize the number of females with which it has the opportunity to mate.

in clusters on huge, isolated trees that nest-robbing monkeys find difficult to reach without becoming vulnerable themselves. In addition, Robinson found that large aggregations of females are most effective at mobbing the Cuvier's toucans and black caracaras that try to rob the nests.

The male caciques provide no parental care; they simply dominate other males and try to mate with as many females as possible during the breeding season. Robinson calls such a mating system "dominance-defence polygyny" or "female-defence polygyny." It is not quite the same as "harem-defence polygyny" because the females are defended one at a time. The male associates with and guards a female until egg laying is finished, then it fights with other males attempting to consort with another female about to breed. Large males in good condition mate with a series of females throughout the breeding season.

As one might expect, this mating system distinctly favours the strongest males, and sexual selection has made male caciques relatively big. In terms of body size, they are among the most sexually dimorphic of all birds, with males being twice as large as females.

Extreme sexual dimorphism and the absence of male parental care are also important in lekking, the most spectacular form of polygyny. The system is a kind of "pure dominance polygyny." A few males are polygynous solely because they are able to dominate and out-display the other males. All that the females receive from lekking males is their sperm and the opportunity to choose a mate from the congregation. Since females receive no male

resources in a lek system, how they maximize their reproductive success is of considerable interest. Studies of lekking birds such as the sage grouse indicate that females are most attracted to males with the highest rates of display and with positions of priority within the lek arena.

In his studies of the Guianan cock-of-the-rock, Pepper Trail of the California Academy of Sciences analyzed female behaviour and found that the females observe the males carefully, visiting several mating courts. They prefer courts clustered near other courts to those that are peripheral or isolated – a preference that would increase their sample of males. They mated with high-ranking males and rejected low-ranking males, which suggested to Trail that females discriminate between males and actively make choices.

Lekking appears to be highly correlated with ecological situations in which males are unable to monopolize something useful to females and where male parental care is not necessary. In the tropical lowlands, egg-eating predators include a panoply of monkeys, opossums and procyonids, as well as snakes and nest-robbing birds. As a result, many tropical birds lower the risk of losing a large clutch by laying only one or two eggs. If that clutch is lost, a new one can be rapidly laid. The small clutch sizes reduce the necessity for male parental care, especially when food is easily obtainable.

Lekking is characteristic of fruit-eating tropical-lowland birds such as manakins and cotingids. The lower-elevation cotingids often have bright, conspicuous males that lek and provide no parental care. Females usually lay only one egg in a flimsy nest.

Given such a small clutch and the availability of easily harvested fruit, male parental care may be unnecessary. The monogamous cotingid species tends to breed on the cold upper slopes of South American mountains where male parental care is more important than it is for the cotingid species which breeds in the lowlands. A relatively large clutch of three eggs is laid in a substantial, well-insulated nest, and males participate in incubation and nest duties. The increased thermal demands of breeding on the colder upper Andean slopes, coupled with a lower predation rate and larger clutch sizes, probably favours monogamy and greater male parental care.

Ordering the mating rites of birds into these kinds of systems is not done simply to pigeonhole nature. The virtue of describing a pattern in such a behaviour as the lekking

disturbs our view of the world. But unless we have some sense of order to contradict, we miss the creative stimulus that comes from being puzzled. When I learned that male quetzals are, in fact, monogamous, I was forced to consider the other factors which might account for the strange combination of flamboyance and parental-care monogamy. Perhaps the answer lies in the fact that quetzals are cavity nesters and may require male-female territorial defence to repel other birds competing for the same nest hole.

Exceptions like quetzals are sometimes the species that best prove a rule. Biologists most often choose to study a species that does not fit a general pattern. That is certainly what has attracted people to the rarest mating system, "classical polyandry," which is the reverse of parental-care polygyny. A female monopolizes several males, which generally provide all the incubation services while the female defends a large territory and forages. Polyandrous birds, including a variety of sandpipers, snipes, phalaropes, moorhens and American jacanas, are predominantly birds of productive and wet habitats. They have precocial young that are able to feed and fend for themselves upon hatching. These features allow males to do most of the parenting. They need only to incubate, and the chicks are soon able to survive on their own. Male incubation and the high productivity of the habitat free the female to produce more than one clutch.

Sometimes, the female will brood the second clutch, but in many species, such as the jacana, the clutch may be left in the care of a male while the female goes on to make another. As with the harem-forming redwinged blackbird males, the reproductive ambitions of jacana females are limited by their ability to defend a territory that includes several males within its bounds. There is a satisfying pattern in the form, colour and behaviour of polyandrous females, which have adopted many of the traits evolved by polygynous males. Polyandrous females are usually larger than the males, more brightly coloured and more

tendency of the cotingids, manakins and birds of paradise is that it helps explain the enigmas of nature.

The first time I saw male resplendent quetzals, I assumed they were highly polygynous birds. I knew that they ate a diet composed largely of fruit and that they were considered to be one of the most spectacular birds in the western hemisphere. My first view of them was of two males displaying in

a clearing of a cloud forest. They alternately raced skyward and then plunged down to the ground one after the other. The conspicuousness of their yard-long tails streaming iridescent emerald, their bellies blazing red and their wild display all suggested lekking. But my expectation was contradicted. I later learned that quetzal males are highly monogamous and parental.

Contradiction intrigues us because it

pugnacious. Female jacanas, for example, can be 75 percent heavier than males, and they can be seen flailing their sharp, spur-armed wings at other females in disputes over territorial boundaries. The role reversal in appearance and parental care is a gratifying confirmation of the prediction that the appearance of the bird is related to its mating system.

The satisfaction that is derived from identifying patterns in avian mating behaviour does not come without a price; the jargon of mating-system biology contains many a daunting phrase. Although naturalists still regard it as a foreign language, we must begin to stutter and stammer it as best we can. Aristotle once argued that thought is impossible without an image. I believe that a related statement is also valid: we need a system of words and patterns to clarify and to retain the images of nature.

The language of behavioural ecology has a catalytic and unifying effect. It allows us to perceive previously unsuspected associations between birds and their environment, such as the one between their colours and their mating systems. It links jacanas treading water lilies and hyacinths with redwings in the cattail marsh. In wetlands bubbling with the sulphurous odour of fecundity and swarming with dragonflies and midges, I have seen, heard and smelled the combination of productivity and polygyny, of precocity and polyandry. I want to remember such experiences with as much clarity as possible. And I believe that the colours of these things remain more vivid, that the smell lingers more pungently, that the dance is livelier because there are words and patterns to capture them.

A male great egret stands guard over its nestlings (far left). Monogamous male birds have evolved behaviour that promotes the survival of their offspring rather than the quantity of their mating opportunities. Female mallard ducks bear the complete burden of care for their ducklings (above). The male's parental investment is negligible; male mallards are notorious for the time they spend trying to forcibly copulate with females.

COLONIES

How birds benefit from the company they keep

The king penguin rookery on South Georgia Island (left) is typical of most seabird colonies, which are most often located on isolated spots where terrestrial predators are few and there is an abundant supply of food nearby.

For years, I took great blue herons for granted. Standing solitary and aloof at the edges of lakes and beaver ponds, they were elegant fixtures of the shoreline, as right as the cedar trees and rushes, and I found them perfectly appropriate for this role. In fact, they seemed a measure of my own intrusiveness, judging the care of my canoe strokes as I passed by, taking flight if I clumsily rapped the gunwale or churned the water. There was nothing about these birds that did not seem natural. Only much later, when I visited their nests, did the habits of the great blues seem odd.

Home for great blue herons in eastern Ontario is usually a stark, beaver-flooded forest, a habitat that in itself is compellingly strange. In summer, when the rest of the world is green and growing, the legions of desolate, grey tree skeletons rising out of the water, crowned with huge bristly platforms of branches, create an apocalyptic feeling. And when the herons fly in at dusk, their two-yard-wide wings beating ponderously against a violet-grey sky, their heads and necks pulled back into a tight S-shape and their long bills issuing harsh "aaaawwk" cries, they are reminiscent of pterodactyls.

Although the birds live in colonies, I have never detected a trace of conviviality in the scene. A naturalist watching the heronry from a darkening hillside senses it must be something other than amicability that brings great blues together.

The coloniality of the great blues troubles the mind because it seems ill-suited to the rest of their life history and behaviour. The herons breed as monogamous pairs and do not socialize much with their neighbours in the colony. When they set out to forage, they go alone. Little foraging is done around the colony, and each morning, all the birds must fan out from a central point in their daily search for food. Like suburban dwellers who drive long distances into urban centres to make their living, the herons find that commuting is costly in both time and energy; it would be far easier to nest on lone snags here and there near foraging areas.

Great blue herons (above) establish colonies in flooded beaver swamps and other areas where there is an abundance of large dead trees. The supply of nest sites is often limited and therefore the object of fierce competition. The precipitous cliffs of Canada's northern coastlines, meanwhile, offer a haven for millions of seabirds, such as gannets (far right).

Colony life is a popular strategy used by about one-eighth of all bird species. Colonies are often situated in areas such as cliffs and islands that afford protection from terrestrial predators. Nevertheless, the colonial habit is mysterious because the gregariousness it demands is out of proportion to apparent necessity. We observe tens of thousands of seabirds packed onto one cliff while miles of likely coastline stand empty, and we marvel at the stressful congestion the birds have chosen in the midst of vast areas of unused space.

In his book *The Secret Islands*, naturalist Franklin Russell gives an especially vivid account of the squalor and confusion of a murre colony on Funk Island, off the northern coast of Newfoundland. The island gets its name from the odour produced by the concentration of excrement, exploding addled eggs, regurgitated fish, dead nestlings—in short, "the stench of a million creatures packed together in a small place." Russell was overwhelmed by the gases, by the sound of the murres and by the sight of the sky dancing with 100,000 swirling birds, and he concludes his impression of the oppressive confusion by commenting that "the struggling homuncular forms piled together in such utter, inhuman chaos denied any ordered view of the universe."

An orderly view may seem out of reach for the naturalist faced with the pandemonium of brute rock, the smell of sulphides and salt wind, the sounds of murres and their exploding eggs; but it can all be reduced to the relationship between such chaos and the need for individual reproductive success. The individual within a colony should live there only if the crowding raises its reproductive success beyond the level that it could achieve by living alone.

Bird colonies are inherently impressive, but biologists study them for more than their bustling character. Familiar with the human disadvantages of overcrowding, they observe bird colonies and wonder what the attraction of such high-density living could be for wild species. Certainly, we find nature most fascinating when we stumble upon a phenomenon that does not quite fit into the standard preconceived mould.

When a young Charles Darwin came across seashells buried high in the Andes Mountains, miles above the sea, he knew his find did not fit the existing theories of science. By paying close attention to such anomalies and developing theories about them, Darwin was able to revolutionize scientific thought. His approach is an apt one for the naturalist. The rough edges of

Unlike dispersed nesting birds, colonial nesters such as puffins (above) have restricted foraging opportunities. A large number set out from one spot and search the same areas of the ocean for food. The isolation of the gentoo penguin colony ensures that it is relatively free of terrestrial predators; but nest-robbing birds, such as the skua (top right) making off with a penguin egg, are regular visitors. One of the advantages of coloniality is that a mobbing attack is more effective and less risky than a solo defensive effort; a group of royal terns (left) collectively harass an approaching laughing gull.

nature, like the awkwardness of a great blue heronry or a million murres crammed into a stinking ghetto of their own making, are the signposts we must follow when we seek new interpretations of the natural order. After weighing the costs of such crowding, the naturalist can set about understanding the benefits that determine the behaviour.

The disadvantages that come with coloniality are many. Colonial birds head the list of harbourers of vermin. Ornithologists Miriam Rothschild and Teresa Clay, writing about bird parasites, proclaim, "By far, the most uncomfortable nests are those of the sand martin." The martins nest close together and return to the same colony site year after year. And each spring, a new generation of thousands of fleas hungry for the blood of their hosts anticipates the return of the swallows, gathering eagerly at the neat circular holes in the ground, the entrances to the swallows' nest chambers. Naturalist Gilbert White was probably the first to notice the phenomenon, remarking in a letter dated February 26, 1774, "This

species of swallow, moreover, is strangely annoyed with fleas; and we have seen fleas, bedfleas (*Pulex irritans*), swarming at the mouths of these holes, like bees on the stools of their hives."

In addition to the presence of parasites and disease, crowding seems to increase both the destruction of eggs and the death rate of chicks. Gulls are notorious for pecking and killing any strange chicks that wander nearby, and chicks that are displaced from their nests or roam usually die this way in dense gull colonies. In cliff-swallow communities, females often dump their eggs into the nests of others; in effect, parasitizing their parental care.

A dense concentration of colonial birds also makes piracy profitable for other birds. Around puffin colonies, skuas cruise back and forth waiting for puffins to return with fish in their bills. By harassing a puffin in flight, the skua forces it to drop its fish. The more puffins there are returning to a specific area, the more profitable it will be for skuas to specialize in robbing puffins. In other

The bright pink American, or Caribbean, flamingos (left) breed in concentrations that are related to their specialized foraging ecology and to the relatively uncommon habitats they frequent. They breed close to where they feed, in shallow salt lagoons where the small organisms they sieve from the mud and water occur in great abundance. Seabirds such as these chinstrap penguins (above) can form massively large colonies because of the incredibly high food production of the southern oceans.

words, if puffins dispersed their burrows and were not colonial, skuas would not be able to rob them as easily, and each puffin would keep more of its catch.

Predation Pressure

When a crow flies toward a colony of red-winged blackbirds, hundreds of eyes intercept its approach. An alarm call almost instantly alerts all the birds in the vicinity. A mobbing call sends dozens of red-winged blackbirds aloft. They dive on the hapless crow, driving it from the area. A crow might easily ignore or evade a single songbird, but when half a dozen attack, it must go on its way. I have seen mobbing songbirds actually strike a fleeing crow from above, causing feathers to fly. And I have been struck in the back of the head by a redwing male while another redwing distracted me by hovering nearby. For the same reason, I can never approach a nesting tern colony—the combined assault of the terns is too intimidating.

Tony Gaston and David Nettleship of the Canadian Wildlife Service have studied murre colonies and have seen some of the strategies murres use to resist predators. In their study, they watched glaucous gulls use two techniques to get at murre eggs and nestlings. On wide and thinly populated ledges, the gulls simply landed and attacked the murres directly, an approach that was not possible when the murres were massed together. But they also sailed in along the cliff, grabbed the wing of a defending murre parent and yanked it off the ledge. By the time the murre was able to gain flight and circle back, its egg or chick was gone. The tactic was dependent upon population density. Murres are not passive in the face of gull attacks. They sound an alert call, "uggah" or "owka," and orient en masse toward the gulls, some pecking or lunging at the attackers. When opposed by a tight phalanx of bills, gulls are usually unsuccessful.

But the notion of a city fortress does not fit the tremendous variation in colony size that exists in thick-billed murres or other colonial birds. Why should colonies of hundreds of thousands of birds exist? They cannot offer greater protection than do colonies of 10,000, and yet they must strain local resources incredibly. Nor does predation pressure seem to explain why birds like great blue herons, which appear to face no nest-threatening predator, form colonies. Indeed, herons suffer most from nest takeovers by other herons attempting to join the heronry.

With the absence of predation pressure in such cases, we are left wondering what pressure it is that packs the birds together into such immensely congested aggregations. Gaston and others have suggested that it is the need for information.

That novel interpretation was proposed in 1973 by ornithologists Peter Ward and Amotz Zahavi; and in 1974, John Krebs of Oxford University followed with a study supporting the notion that great blue heron colonies exist as information centres that herons use to increase their ability to find food. Krebs proposed that the birds live in colonies because they can watch other herons flying back to their nests with food and also detect the direction these successful individuals take on their next trip.

Gaston argues that the information-centre concept helps account for the pattern of variation in the size of thick-billed murre colonies in the eastern Canadian Arctic. Murres populate the area in summer, exploiting the rich schools of Arctic cod and crustaceans and breeding on the steep thousand-foot cliffs of Baffin and Prince Leopold islands. The cliff faces offer safety from nest-robbing animals like the Arctic fox. But what has puzzled Gaston is the fact that while 1.5 million murres cram themselves into a mere 10 colonies, the smallest of which contains 10,000 murres, much smaller colonies exist farther south.

The difference in food resources between the north and the south does not support the idea that food-resource concentration allows for larger northern colonies. Nor does increased predation pressure seem to favour larger northern colonies. Instead, Gaston's studies show that the larger colonies occur where pack-ice movement is unpredictable. Changes in the wind and current can move miles of ice cover within one or two days; murres in these areas sometimes have to fly 60 miles on each foraging trip. Because the costs of heading in a wrong direction are tremendous, the value of information about food locations is increased.

Successful foragers among murre populations depart without attempting to join an outgoing flock. But other murres waiting

The swirling cacophony of a cloud of elegant terns (far left) and the risk of head-battering attacks from all sides persuade many intruders to leave the vicinity of a tern colony. Another aspect of life in a communal roost is its function as an information centre. The blackbirds (above) can tag along with other more experienced birds to food sites. Thick-billed murres (right) likewise increase their foraging success by making use of the flight-path information of incoming birds, which enables inexperienced foragers to target their search.

below the cliffs tag along behind these birds, eventually arranging themselves in huge V-shaped formations and heading off to feeding areas as much as two hours' flying time away. A group consisting of only a few birds might lack information about food locations, but in colonies of tens of thousands, there should be enough coverage of the thousands of miles of ocean for incoming successful birds to orient the unsuccessful birds. The smaller murre colonies exist in areas of open water, where flight and search costs are not as severe.

There is always a trade-off at work: if the colony grows too large, the benefit of the information may be outweighed by local food depletion. Gaston has found that in an intermediate-sized colony, young murres leaving the colony weigh 8.5 ounces, while in a huge colony of 300,000, the chicks reach only 5.5 ounces before they must leave the area. He suggests that increased foraging success favours larger colonies in areas of unpredictable food supply but that, eventually, local depletion of the food supply restricts the size of the colony.

Information Transfer

As with any new idea, the onus is on its advocates to demonstrate its validity. One skeptical ornithologist, Roger Evans of the University of Manitoba, has insisted that "to confirm the information-centre hypothesis and its importance, proponents must document information exchange directly and show that information exchange at a colony is not rare."

That has now been done. Charles Brown of Yale University has recently shown that cliff-swallow colonies are indeed information centres for the swallows. Cliff swallows are potential candidates for such a phenomenon because of their breeding and feeding ecology. The gourdlike mud nests they build are packed together on cliff faces, bridges and other large structures, and the swallows breed in tight proximity and in synchrony. More important, their food supply is patchy and unreliable. The swallows feed on swarms of insects, often dense clouds of mating midges. The swarms can be incred-

ibly rich, thick enough to feed more than 500 swallows at a time, but they are rapidly depleted and rarely last more than half an hour. When the cloud is consumed or disperses, the swallows must range over the landscape searching for a new source.

One way a disappointed searcher might increase its foraging success would be to keep an eye out as successful swallows return to the colony and to follow as they depart. Brown and a group of field assistants set out to observe cliff swallows in Nebraska, where the treeless terrain and the sheer numbers of swallows provided ideal conditions. They examined an amazing number of cliff-swallow colonies, 167 in all, which varied in size from 2 to 3,000 nests.

Successful foragers returned with their mouths and throats packed full and rocked back and forth in a characteristic way as they discharged the food into the nest. Unsuccessful returning birds simply sat quietly at the nest. There was an obvious difference in the behaviour of the two classes of birds. Unsuccessful birds were five times more likely to follow a darting bird as was a successful forager. Using binoculars, observers could see the followers accompanying the successful foragers as they flew back to a swarm of insects. Just as important, the followers did not simply tail after any departing bird. They selectively followed birds that had previously arrived with food, preferring them by a margin of 10 to 1 over unsuccessful birds. Following was a tactic that all birds seemed to rely on.

The transfer of information was not necessarily voluntary or cooperative. The simplest interpretation is that individuals in a colony profited by observing other in-

Cliff swallows (far left) aggregate in groups and build their nests well beyond the reach of most predators. But they may also aggregate because they feed on short-lived insects whose presence is unpredictable. When one swallow finds a swarm of insects and returns to the colony, the other birds can take advantage of the discovery and follow the successful forager as it leaves the colony once again. Painted storks (above) often nest near each other yet are intolerant of other storks attempting to exploit information about food sources.

Although bald eagles (above) will not nest next to other pairs of bald eagles, they often roost and feed communally in areas of high food abundance during the winter. Ospreys (far right), however, have flexibility in their nesting behaviour. In inland areas, they may nest in isolation, while in rich coastal bays, they may gather in loose colonies.

dividuals that were successful at finding a food patch. And since the availability of food was so unpredictable, virtually all birds had to follow others at some time or another.

As naturalists, we now have a link between the costs and benefits of life in a swallow colony. When the midges begin to hover above a shrub at dusk, the sudden appearance of swallows is all the more remarkable to us, for as the swallows reap their harvest with every looping pass, their reward is put into perspective for us by the knowledge that their meals are the up side of a flea-ridden coloniality.

New insights into the operation of osprey colonies by Erick Greene of Princeton University recently reminded me of my capacity to underestimate a bird's abilities. I had not thought of ospreys as colonial, because where I live, they are widely dispersed on

the tops of isolated white pines. But Greene, studying a colony of ospreys in Nova Scotia, revealed just how limited my conception of the osprey's life history was.

Ospreys often nest in clusters, some colonies containing 300 pairs. Greene found a colony of seven pairs, all within 50 yards of each other, that could be observed from a bluff overlooking the nests and the bay. The view allowed both Greene and, apparently, the ospreys to note the identity of the fish being carried into the colony by successful foragers.

Usually, the ospreys returned with winter flounder, pollack, alewife or smelt, and the kind of fish seemed to influence subsequent departures by other birds. Ospreys that left when a successful hunter returned chose to fly off in the direction from which the incoming fish-bearer had arrived. By contrast, birds without access to the information borne by successful hunters flew off in virtually random directions. The ospreys that headed off in the direction of returning successful birds also based their behaviour on the type of catch they observed.

Winter flounder, understandably, did not generally induce flight, because information about the location of one flounder does not indicate that another flounder will also be found there. But since smelt, pollack and alewives travel in dense schools, information on school location is potentially valuable. The ospreys left rapidly, flying in the direction of the successful catcher of any of these three species. But did the spying actually benefit the information-gathering birds? Greene found that birds with access to information about the schooling fish returned with a catch in 10 minutes; the same birds without information sometimes spent up to an hour searching. As expected, informed and naïve birds did not differ in their ability to find winter flounder.

Greene's study is proof of the sophistication with which birds can evaluate information and use it to increase their foraging success. It is also proof of the value of looking beyond the status quo in search of anomalies in nature and examining them from a variety of perspectives.

For centuries, humans have seen birds in colonies and simply assumed that that was how certain birds lived. Theories about information being used by birds for their own benefit came about only after scientists had declared information as a human resource worthy of being measured, classified, stored, transmitted, stolen and protected. Although information science flourished in the 1930s and 1940s, it took several decades before the first theoretical application to avian coloniality was made in 1973. Another 15 years passed before any significant research reinforced the theory.

As exciting a discovery as it is, the link between coloniality and information exchange gives us something larger to ponder. As a biologist, I consider Greene's discovery an important breakthrough, but as a naturalist, I am made even more painfully aware

of how our knowledge is limited to what we are. We understand much about bird song because we are musical; we know about avian sociality because we are social; the language of plumage and display has been extensively studied because humans are visual beings.

We also know that there are important aspects of avian life that will elude us forever. It took us centuries to discover the information/coloniality link. We know that we will continue to learn more and more about birds simply because our beliefs and ideas continue to change and grow. Nevertheless, I cannot help chafing at the time it takes for science to enlarge our view.

As I watch the evening traffic of great blue herons bound for their nests, I wonder what still passes me by, silent and out of sight, unthought of and unknown.

PROPAGANDA
Whole truths, half truths and outright lies

The threatening posture of the bald eagle (left) defending its catch of salmon reveals design features that contribute to its intimidating effect: the eagle's powerful bill is emphasized, and the spread of its shoulders increases the impact of the bird's size.

In the white pine above me was a group of jays; one of them issued a soft stream of sounds. I crept closer until I could hear the jay clearly, but its burbling still had no meaning for me. Then the muttering jay saw me and let loose a more familiar outburst—a loud, braying "jay, jay, jay, jay." I had no difficulty in understanding that: the simplest translation was "intruder, intruder!" The signal was picked up by the other jays in the flock, and they sailed away to safety.

When I am able to interpret a bird call, I get a smug feeling of satisfaction. For a moment, the apparently garbled languages of nature make sense. That is one reason for waiting under the white pines, resisting the urge to swat prospecting mosquitoes—to stalk the stimulus and response, hoping to glimpse the mind of a bird.

My interpretation of the jay's call may seem like a simple cause-and-effect deduction. But making the deduction depends heavily on our beliefs about the purpose of communication and behaviour. The "jay, jay" call seems to fit the conventional hu-man sense of communication. Humans say "we communicate well" to indicate understanding, while the statement "we aren't communicating" acknowledges a barrier to understanding. In other words, we assume communication is a cooperative act during which useful information is transmitted and received. The blue jay warns its flock mates by cawing, and all the birds benefit.

One of the most respected students of avian communication, Peter Marler of New York City's Rockefeller University, has written that "communication in the fullest sense implies evolutionary specialization of a mutualistic, cooperative nature"; he has also characterized communication as an interplay between participants that are each committed to making the interchange as efficient as possible. John Smith, another specialist in bird communication, who defines communication as the sharing of information between or among individuals, suggests that the function of bird displays is to "make the behaviour of the communicator more predictable to a recipient." Such

"Get out of here," they have jeered, and I have gone.

The alteration of my behaviour by the jays embodies much of the biological essence of communication. The jay's evolutionary interest lies in controlling my behaviour for its own personal benefit. Communications of this sort are better viewed as messages designed to influence and manipulate the recipients in a way that benefits their sender. In other words, "communication" is very nearly a synonym for "propaganda"; that is, the material and persuasive methods used to convert an audience. The truthfulness of propaganda is less important than its function, which is to be convincing.

Evolutionary Suicide

And where does this take science? Consider the alarm call, that unambiguous cry of the jay or of any songbird. If we conceive of communication as a cooperative venture, then it is easy to assume that the alarm call functions as a warning to a bird's neighbours. Countless texts have explained it thusly. But listen again to that bird — the one that sounds the alarm. You have turned your head to find the bird and watch it whistle. Why should that particular bird risk your hungry gaze and draw the attention of a predator to itself while its neighbours, its genetic and ecological competitors, benefit from its alertness? Such altruism would be evolutionary suicide.

Until behavioural biologists began to think of the adaptive significance that behaviour held for individuals rather than species, alarm calls were not evolutionarily interesting acts. The best work on alarm calls was done 30 years ago by Peter Marler. His elegant physical analysis showed how songbird alarm calls were acoustically easy for other small birds to hear and difficult for large predators to locate. No one had questioned why a seemingly altruistic behaviour had evolved in the first place. Biologists had simply not thought about the adaptive significance of alarm calling.

Since then, several theories have argued that alarm calls are given not to aid recipients of the call at all but to benefit the bird

an interpretation of communication implies that it evolves in a way that facilitates understanding. According to this view, communication is a cooperative event involving the predictable, efficient exchange of information. If that were true, the task of the naturalist would be simplified.

Before we can understand bird behaviour, we must consider why birds are communicating. If we pause to think evolutionarily, we expect that an individual communicates because it is in its best interest to do so. Natural selection will favour organisms which communicate in ways that increase their reproductive success, which is why Harvard University sociobiologist E.O. Wilson defines biological communication as "the action on the part of one organism (or cell) that alters the probability pattern of behaviour of another organism (or

cell) in a fashion adaptive to one or both of the participants."

These ideas change the way the naturalist perceives and reacts to birds. Listen again to that jay. Its eyes are looking at yours, it hops about the branches overhead and caws raucously. It is communicating with you, but it has no intention of cooperating. Its message may be a discouraging "I have seen you, and I know where you are, so forget about trying to make a meal of me" or perhaps "Get lost, or my incessant noise will alert every other possible meal in the area of your whereabouts." More than once, I have been moved by such hectoring to grab a fallen branch or a fistful of acorns and fling it at the jays. But more often, I have left an area to get away from a noisy flock. Their simple bird brains have had no difficulty in forcing me to do exactly as they intended.

that does the calling. One of the theories is that the first bird to spot a predator possesses information which it can then use for its own good. It knows the location of the predator; its flock mates do not. By calling, it causes other birds to move and thereby reduces its own chances of being attacked by the predator. Alternatively, the caller might deter pursuit by indicating its awareness of the predator. Another possibility is that the bird might call selectively, depending on whether close kin such as offspring or a mate are in the vicinity.

Kimberly Sullivan of Rutgers University in New Jersey used this new perspective to examine the alarm-calling behaviour of some common wintering birds in eastern deciduous forests, including black-capped chickadees, tufted titmice and downy woodpeckers. These birds often form mixed flocks that travel together through the forest to forage. Regularly preyed upon by an assortment of raptors, they all give alarm calls and react to each other's warnings by freezing or taking evasive action. Sullivan observed the natural interactions between raptors and banded, sexed birds in foraging flocks, and she simulated interactions by experimental presentations of hawk models.

Chickadees and titmice made the vast majority of alarm calls, with chickadees calling virtually every time a hawk was encountered. By contrast, downy woodpeckers never called when foraging alone or when the other downies present were of the same sex. Calls were most often given when a male and female were foraging together. The simplest interpretation of their behaviour—that the downies gave alarm calls to warn their mates—accounts for the

The male marsh wren (far left) uses the size of its song repertoire to impress rivals and mates. Since song repertoires are learned rather than instinctive behaviour, the singer of many songs is providing information about its age and learning ability. The gliding herring gull (above) communicates courtship intentions with a distinctive mewing call.

89

The killdeer (above) manages to distract predators from its nest with a simulated broken-wing display, an obvious but effective example of communication involving manipulative propaganda. The threat display of the young great horned owl (far right) includes a combination of bluffing elements, such as the wing spreading that exaggerates its size. The bill and large talons of the owl are weapons of real power. Communication is often a complex mixture of exaggeration and truthful advertisement.

readiness of black-capped chickadees and titmice to call: their flocks are composed of mated pairs, and the calls were made selectively and self-interestedly.

An even more self-interested and manipulative use of alarm calling has been documented by Charles Munn of the New York Zoological Society. Munn and John Terborgh of Princeton University studied the tremendously complex foraging flocks in the rain forest in the Manú region of Peru. As many as 80 species may participate in the flocks, which are permanent and active all year. Usually, the flocks have a core of 5 to 10 species and specialize in foraging for insects either in the canopy or in the understorey. Munn showed that there is a definite social structure in the flocks which is related to the alarm-calling behaviour of some species.

The canopy foragers were led by white-winged shrike tanagers and the understorey flocks by bluish slate antshrikes. These species also acted as sentinels, being the first birds to call loudly when a bird-eating hawk was spotted. Munn's most exciting discovery was that the sentinel birds cry "hawk" both honestly and dishonestly.

The sentinel species ate large insects such as katydids and relied on the activities of other flock members to flush such prey out into the open. The sentinel bird and another flock member often found themselves in pursuit of the same flying insect. Under these conditions, the sentinel bird gave a false alarm call. Munn believes that caused the sentinel's rival for the flying roach or katydid to hesitate, which neatly gave the sentinel an advantage in the chase. Because somewhat more than half of the alarm calls honestly signalled the presence of a hawk, the rival bird could not afford to ignore the sentinel's warning; the insect's value was small compared with life itself. The asymmetry in knowledge and the cost of ignoring a warning enabled the sentinel bird to manipulate and deceive its flock mates when it was advantageous to do so.

Deceptive Practices

Being able to tune in to bird communication and to see and hear its sophistication depends on our recognizing that birds are capable of deceptive practices. For those who still doubt that a mere bird is capable of deception, I suggest you take a walk in a gravelly open field where killdeers are nesting. The male will intercept an intruder with pathetic whinnying cries. His wing flap will appear to be broken and useless as he runs. His tail will bend down to expose a rump of reddish orange that looks as if it is matted with blood; he is a helpless bird, ready to be silenced and eaten.

We are not fooled. We have heard that killdeers behave in such a manner, and so we oblige the bird and let it go through its motions. But our understanding of the display does not diminish its significance. It is a demonstration of an organism broadcasting misleading information. More important, the bird willfully displays; it is manifestly a living being beaming out signals in an effort to alter our behaviour.

We are not always so consciously prepared that we are immune to manipulation. A few summers ago, I unwittingly blundered near a grouse hen and her chicks. The hen came running out of the shrubbery straight at me, with her wings akimbo and her neck feathers flared out in a threat. And even though the bird was bluffing a much larger being, the bluff worked. I was stopped in my tracks by the sudden mock assault.

The grouse's bluff worked as well as it did because it came close to the boundary that separates communication and direct action. Those who study communication like to make a distinction between the two. One example I enjoy is the difference between

telling someone to jump off a cliff (an interaction that constitutes communication) and simply throwing the person off (something that does not qualify as communication). The distinction highlights the symbolic nature of communication.

A symbol, by definition, is a sign or an act that represents something else. A male rooster can communicate a threat to a rival cock with calls and spreading of feathers, sometimes following up with a violent attack. The aggressive call and feather display can evolve as a symbolic device for communicating aggressive intent. If we are to understand bird communication, we have to recognize that birds use symbols in communication just as humans do, employing displays and structures to signal information about features such as sexual identity, age, strength and dominance status.

The symbols birds use must always be treated with skepticism because they are indirect and potentially falsifiable propaganda. Owning a large, expensive car may symbolize either great wealth or great debt; the symbol must be checked against other indicators. The same is true of bird displays. For example, male red-winged blackbirds wear a status symbol on their wings. The red and yellow epaulets denote a mature male ready to breed. Immature males, normally unable to defend a territory, lack the conspicuous bright badge.

Some birds feather out into fully adult plumage following their first moult. But redwings, along with indigo buntings, scarlet tanagers and some 30 other North American songbirds, have delayed plumage maturation, which means that first-year males usually have duller epaulets and do not normally develop brilliant badges until their second year. The delay occurs even though they are physiologically capable of breeding and possess well-developed testes and viable sperm.

But if pigment is all it takes to make a status symbol, why don't the yearling males simply fake it? Why don't young males develop the hormones and enzymes needed to create the coloured status badges and thereby enjoy the genetic rewards of high status? Several studies have indicated that bluffing might be adaptive, because it is possible to raise the status of a bird simply by painting it with the colours of dominance. Seifert Rohwer of the University of Washington and Doris Watt of the University of Notre Dame have both experimented with the dark throat markings of Harris's sparrows. The plumage patterns are distinctive, allowing for individual recognition, and the extent of the dark pigment increases with age. Juveniles given dark paint spots around their throats were able to dominate their lighter-coloured peers. Under natural conditions, however, birds will be challenged not only by their peers but also by older, more experienced birds, which would clearly limit the value of bluffing.

Birds use plumage badges to assess territorial and fighting status. If the badges of a territorial male red-winged blackbird are covered, it becomes subject to increasing numbers of challenges from males that have not been previously able to acquire and hold a territory. Apparently, they react as though the altered male is immature and possessed of limited fighting ability. However, the altered males are usually able to win their battles despite their perceived vulnerability, indicating that the badge normally signals the territorial ability associated with maturity.

In this sense, avian displays and signs of status are analogous to a poker game. When a player makes a bid, the other players do not simply accept it at face value. The challenger assesses the hand by a variety of methods, one of which is to raise the ante. The game is a mixture of signalling ploys and probing assessments. If you watch male redwings at a marsh in spring, you will see them displaying their status badges in a similar manner. The male corroborates his colourful advertisement with a lusty "conk-a-ree" call and boldly spreads his wings. Other males swoop past, and he must give chase, or they will turn back on him and force him to fight. If at any stage his actions are not convincing, his rivals will escalate the contest until a winner is decided.

Scott Freeman of the University of Washington has shown that male redwings assess the fighting ability of other males by watching how they respond to threats. He presented model male redwings to territory holders and recorded how vigorously the territory holder attacked the intruding model. The presentations were conducted in a way that allowed neighbouring redwing males to observe the conflict between the model and the defender. Birds that failed to launch a vigorous attack on the model subsequently suffered a much higher rate of challenge and intrusion than they had prior to the presentation of the model. By contrast, the males that attacked the model did not receive more intrusions on their territory than normal, which suggests that if redwings perceive any sign of weakness in their neighbours, they take advantage of it to expand their territory.

Because a status symbol may be either an honest signal or mere propaganda, we expect birds to evolve mechanisms for skeptical assessment. Redwing males, for example, are fighters, and individuals that advertise falsely risk injury if they cannot defend themselves effectively when challenged. Bruce Lyon of Princeton University and Bob Montgomerie of Queen's University at Kingston have suggested that dull plumage is an honest signal of subordinate status. A dull male is less likely to be attacked by an older and more formidable bright male. Since young males are poor fighters, this signal reduces their risk of injury. When a bird does possess exceptional abilities, then it is in its interest to evolve a means of making its attributes obvious, which will serve not only to forestall challenges from rivals but also to attract mates.

Unambiguous Message

I have listened to three-wattled bellbirds issue their clanging calls all day long in the Costa Rican cloud forest. These birds are thought to call louder than any other bird on Earth. In earlier times, I would have viewed the males as merely hormonally programmed beacons calling out their identity with a distinctive high-decibel call designed to reach females in the muffled, mossy forest. But when I began paying attention to different individuals, the powerful signal also exhibited variations in tone and intensity. Young bellbirds, especially, gave a pathetic call—a raspy soprano squeak compared with the rich tenor clang of more mature males. Ornithologist Michael Fogden estimates that it takes bellbird males as long as four years to develop the mature high-decibel signal.

It is the female that makes the variation in calling ability significant. A female bellbird scouting for a male swoops in and sits beside him on his perch. He turns toward her, and if he has the required vigour, he "bonks" full in her face so hard that he blows her off the branch. The loudly clanging male, then, is proclaiming ability and age in a reliable manner.

There are many other situations in which the signaller benefits from making his message unambiguous, so it is a mistake to overemphasize the manipulative quality of communication. Many bird displays feature postures that have become highly ritualized and are an accurate reflection of intention. One well-studied series of rituals is that of courting male green herons. The male sets up a territory in a dead snag and begins calling out "skow, skow," a signal that probably repels males but attracts females. If a heron lands in the male's tree, the male challenges the new arrival with a full-forward display. Crouching forward, he erects his head crest and puffs out his body feathers. He flips his tail and spreads his bill to reveal a bright red mouth lining; then, with wings flapping, he cries "raaaahhh."

If the spectator is a male, this is his cue to leave. The actor is clearly a male using a display of ritualized fighting, complete with crouch and highlighting of the rapier bill. The display is based on history, a reworking of the motions and implements of battle. If the spectator is female, a convincing display of maleness may induce her to remain. Staying put is interpreted by the displaying male as an indication of a female's willingness to mate, and he switches to a radically different set of postures known as the stretch display. He moves out of the crouch, stands up to expose his bright orange legs, raises his bill in a vertical skyward tilt and sways from side to side while giving a low "aarooo" call.

The design of the stretch display illustrates the "principle of antithesis" struc-

The brilliant epaulet badges of the red-winged blackbird (above) are usually worn only by mature males and are conspicuously displayed during territorial interactions as symbols of age and experience. First-year males often have badges of subdued colour or, like females, may lack them altogether.

93

turing the ritual. To show his courtship intentions, the male offers the antithesis of the signals used to convey aggression. It is in the male's genetic interest to use ritualized and stereotypic motions that clearly convey his intentions toward the female.

Humans, of course, employ the same sort of behaviour. What is the open hand we offer in greeting but the symbolic antithesis of the clenched fist or the hand armed with a weapon? With this gesture, we communicate friendship. But at the same time, we may harbour malicious purposes despite our symbolic gesture. The possible coexistence of truth and fiction in any interaction is what makes communication a complex tactical exercise.

Philosopher Susanne Langer at one time attempted to distinguish between humans and other species by arguing that a human "is not only exposed to those that visibly or tangibly surround him. . . . Even the dead may still play into his life." She goes on to say that "symbolic construction has made [the human being's] vastly involved and extended world, and mental adroitness is his chief asset in exploiting it."

The modern study of avian behaviour has revealed that birds, too, utilize sophisticated symbolic acts. When we watch a bird communicating, we are witnessing an individual influencing its own fate and being influenced by others. In its life, each bird makes its way against a flow of messages and symbols; some are straight truths and others are subtle falsehoods. That is why we can empathize with a bird's struggle to communicate and comprehend. We also travel these difficult rivers of meaning.

Courting birds utilize their bills in courtship displays. The territorial male green heron (above) uses ritualized postures that include changing the position of its long lethal bill to communicate with other green herons, crouching to indicate aggression or raising its head and bill vertically to indicate courtship intentions to females. During breeding season, the broad, colourfully pigmented bills of Atlantic puffins (right) brighten and grow larger.

94

IMAGES
Startled predators and disguised prey

I was wading down the Río Peñas Blancas, a cold clear river in the Tilaran Mountains of Costa Rica. The river gorge had narrowed to a dark canyon of rock. The sun was hidden by the forest leaning over the canyon edges, and the water was a cold, translucent band of roiling blue-green light in the gloom. Ahead was the white glare of a wide sunlit expanse of boulders.

I was concentrating, trying to place my feet securely in the bed of slick, rounded river rock, fighting the tug of the current with each step. As I reached the edge of the dark shadow, a huge face with glowing orange-yellow eyes the size of plates suddenly loomed up over me from behind a boulder. And then, just as suddenly, the image collapsed and sailed away.

It was no hallucination, no forest spirit. I realized I had just seen a sunbittern conjure up the billboard-sized face of an owl, a fierce image six feet wide. It is an illusion that sunbitterns call into existence regularly, an alarming threat display of glaring eyes.

Sunbitterns inhabit lake and river edges in tropical forest areas of Central and South America. As they step along a rushing river, bobbing and rocking, they look strangely like a cross between a heron and a grebe, attractive yet neither remarkable nor intimidating. But whenever one senses danger while sitting on its nest of leaves and mud along a limb overhanging the river, a transformation takes place. In the mottled shade, the slate-grey bird sits inconspicuously until it feels threatened by the approach of another bird or mammal. The sunbittern then lifts up its tail, spreads its wings and turns them forward, flashing the huge sunburst patterns that resemble giant eyes. A loud, grating squawk reinforces the terrorism of the display.

The artwork on the sunbittern's wing is a sophisticated illusion created by ingenious countershading and posturing. When the wing is spread and its feathers fanned out, an "eyeball" is created by juxtaposing a black-rimmed oval of orange with a larger oval area of light yellow. An outer band of

The ash-throated flycatcher (left) leaves its perch to catch flying insects and then returns to the perch to feed. The ability to distinguish between highly evasive and easy-to-catch insects or between poisonous and edible insects at a distance is a crucial determinant of the flycatcher's foraging success.

97

The feathers of the sunbittern (above) are patterned to create concentric, countershaded circles that appear to mimic eyespots which scare off intruders. The Io moth (left) uses a similar technique: when birds peck at it, the moth flips its forewings up to reveal two large false eyespots which resemble those of owls. This display is known to startle insect-eating birds. Predation behaviour usually combines both instinctive and learned responses. The barred owl (far right) caught this mouse by using a mixture of instinctive reactions to stimuli given off by the prey, such as its high-pitched squeaks and rustlings, and learned reactions based on actual experience.

shading hems both sides of the "face" with another set of concentric orange and black curves. The raised tail fills in the centre of the face.

The sunbittern's display is far from a perfect portrait of an owl face. But its sudden flash may be enough to move a nest-robbing bird or opossum out of the area. The display is meant to deceive by exploiting the fact that large eyes often indicate the presence of an owl or other large predator.

The success of eyespots is based on their stunning effect. Victorian naturalist W.H. Hudson wrote about how electrifying owl eyes are to even discerning human observers: "Cats among mammals and owls among birds have been highly favoured; but to owls, the palm must be given. The feline eyes, as of a puma or wild cat blazing with wrath, are wonderful to see; sometimes the sight of them affects one like an electric shock. But for intense brilliance and quick changes, the dark orbs kindling with the startling suddenness of a cloud illuminated by flashes of lightning, the yellow globes of the owl are unparallelled."

Avoidance Response

The effectiveness of the owl-eye device is apparently so strong that it has evolved independently on the hind wings of butterflies and moths, mantids, lantern flies, katydids and click beetles; even fish and frogs have them. Permanently exposed eyespots are used by various butterflies to deflect pecking attacks from vulnerable areas. Other organisms reveal their owl-eye device only in times of threat. Io moths, for example, are highly cryptic when at rest during the day, nestled onto the bark of tree trunks. Their dull fore wings cover hind wings that each bear a large eye. In summer, they are tremendously common in mixed deciduous forest, and yet they are hardly ever observed by day. Birds, however, patrol the tree trunks, and when they encounter a mothlike object, they give it an exploratory peck. The Io moth's response is to flick its fore wings ahead. Two large black and yellow owl eyes suddenly flash into view.

When one is expecting the display, it is hardly frightening, but its effect on a bird at close range is truly remarkable. Studies of the Io have shown that the startle display caused yellow buntings to leap away and fly off in apparent fright. The buntings appear to flee instinctively when the image of an owl is suddenly encountered.

In his wonderful book *One Man's Owl*, Bernd Heinrich, an ecologist at the University of Vermont, mentions that some joggers gain relief from attacks of territorial birds diving at their heads by painting giant eyes on their caps. He also notes that a Japanese airline has applied for a patent on painted owl eyes around its jet engines. The airline had suffered much damage from birds flying into its planes and discovered that the eyes dramatically reduced the frequency of bird strikes.

Evidently, the image of owl eyes has a great currency in-the wild. Throughout a history of harmful encounters with owls, birds have evolved an avoidance response to owl eyes – natural selection has favoured small birds that flee the image of an owl, an image whose essence is large eyes.

Once, while cross-country skiing, I saw a great horned owl perched in a dead elm. It swooped down on a squirrel foraging in the crown of a sugar maple. Prior to its launch, the owl, with its mottled grey coat, must have been hard to detect in the high-contrast combination of bright sunlight, snow and dark trees; only the large round eyes could alert its prey. But on that day, the squirrel reacted too late. The owl snagged it from the branch and carried it to another tree. Alarmed by my approach, the owl dropped the squirrel, and I saw that the bird had dispatched the rodent by driving a talon through its eye into the brain.

It may have been bad luck on the squirrel's part or good technique on the owl's, but in any case, the result was that an owl had eliminated a creature which had not recognized and reacted to its approach quickly enough. Every day of every year, such culling of the slow and unwary goes on – leaving behind a population of individuals with an easily triggered response to large round eyes. The image of owl eyes has found an instinctive residence in the brains of many species of birds and mammals.

And, in turn, the sunbittern and the Io moth – among others – have evolutionarily been able to exploit the ingrained imagery by mimicking the relevant stimuli and flashing them at approaching predators.

Possibly the best way to imagine the

The motmot (above) lives in the tropical American forests rich in poisonous snakes; it readily chases and eats a variety of reptiles, such as this lizard, but instinctively avoids the colour patterns used by lethally venomous coral snakes. The great blue heron (far right) profits greatly when it is able to spear or grab an eel along a northern coast. But if the heron winters along the Pacific Ocean off Central America, it, too, must be able to distinguish edible eels from venomous sea snakes.

impact of a startle display is to examine the riveting effect of a sudden encounter with a snake. More than once, I have jerked back from a shrub or vine, startled by a serpentine form. The response is involuntary and convulsive, and adrenaline flows. After an interval of calm, I have inspected the shrub carefully and found no snake, only a sphinx moth caterpillar imitating a snake. These caterpillars have two large false eyes set back from their true head capsule, and behind the eyes, they have a special set of muscles. When threatened, they pull the muscles in, constricting the body to produce a credible imitation of a viper head; swaying from side to side, they create an uncanny facsimile of a disturbed snake.

The caterpillar's display is designed to repel foraging birds. Birds can be deceived by such displays because there are vipers that appear to specialize in ambushing birds. For the same reason, the display seems equally effective on human neural circuits forged by countless past encounters with poisonous snakes.

Instant Fright

Examining the caterpillar or Io moth, we are left with a kind of wonder at how such crude imitation is able to work its purpose. Speed is of the essence; our eyes detect danger at the speed of light. We jump first and ask later what it was that caught the eye, alerted the brain, fired the nerves and jerked muscles and limbs. Under sudden stress, our brain gives us no time for careful scrutiny. If we are to grasp the reactions and appearance of a bird, it is well to recall this kind of instant snake fright.

Sudden reactions, of necessity, are based on simple patterns and crucial bits of information rather than on the whole picture. A bird must use a restricted number of key features if it is to react quickly. Because the triggers of an innate response are simple, they are easier to mimic than are the stimuli of more complex learned associations.

Exploitation of simple patterns is most effective when the stakes are high and involve lethal creatures such as coral snakes. Susan Smith of Mount Holyoke College, in

Massachusetts, has shown that turquoise-browed motmots are born with an instinctive aversion to the patterns of the coral snake. Motmots commonly eat snakes and are therefore at risk if they attack lethal snakes. I have watched motmots kill their prey, and their method is crude. They carry their victim to a branch and bludgeon it against the tree or stand on it and peck at the head. It is not a lightning strike, and the bird has a great chance of being bitten.

Smith tested the reactions of naïve motmots to potential snake types by presenting wooden dowels painted with bands or stripes of contrasting colours and allowing young motmots to investigate them as though they might be food items. The motmots pecked at green and blue ring patterns, at yellow and red stripes, at dowels that had a plain end combined with a striped end. However, they completely avoided dowels that were painted with red and yellow bands, which mimicked the pattern of coral snakes. Smith also took redwings and blue jays (which live mainly beyond the range of coral snakes and do not prey upon snakes to any extent) and watched as they attacked the red-and-yellow-banded dowels without restraint, indicating no instinctive fear of coral snakes.

The venom of the coral snake is lethally potent, and untutored birds have no opportunity to learn from mistakes. Fortunately for the motmot, the snakes advertise their deadliness with an easily recognizable and conspicuous design. Their beautiful colours and patterns say to the naïve motmot, "Mess with me, and I will kill you." Smith's studies prove that the image and message are engraved in the motmot's genes and that the young motmot needs no tutoring in the subject.

A similar conclusion was reached in Panama by Gloria Caldwell and Roberta Rubinoff of the Smithsonian Institution, who found that hand-reared great egrets, snowy egrets and green-backed herons instinctively avoided lethal yellow-bellied sea snakes. The birds readily attacked plain-coloured eels but tended to avoid black-and-yellow-patterned eels, even though such eels are harmless and edible.

Instinctive aversion to a prey item seems to depend on the potential for death as a consequence of an attack. Assorted wasps, hornets and bees use concentric yellow and black ring patterns to advertise their stinging power — an image that automatically discourages young chickens from preying on them. But other birds, such as redwings and grackles, are not born with an aversion to the striped patterns and only learn its message through experience. As they peck at wasps and bumblebees, they learn that such choices are painful. Even though the lesson hurts them, it is not fatal, and we can assume that a species' reliance on instinct over learning is related to the degree of harm a mistake can cause.

Meanwhile, a wide variety of species has evolved that takes advantage of existing colour patterns and images as defence resources that can be used to dupe predators. The ecological importance of image mimicry was first recognized by Henry Bates, the great 19th-century naturalist, who realized that some species have evolved to take advantage of a resemblance to other less palatable species. As long as the unpalatable individuals exist in sufficient numbers to have conditioned predators to stay away from them, palatable species can mimic those traits successfully. Many nonvenomous snakes, such as king snakes, have evolved the colour patterns of the poisonous coral snakes. The king snakes are thus protected from predation by birds such as motmots.

The images of unpalatable prey that predators develop need not be encoded as instinct in the birds' genes. The images can be sketched anew in the brain of each bird from its learning experiences — the trial-and-error sampling it uses to determine which foods are palatable and which are not. The work of Lincoln and Jane Brower on monarch butterflies and blue jays provides the classic example of a learned avoidance image.

Monarch caterpillars feed on chemically defended milkweed plants that have cardiac glycosides in their tissues. If you pull a leaf

The katydid (above) mimics the shape, colour and venation of leaves so well that it is invisible to the casual passerby. The sophistication of the mimicry is evidence of the evolutionary effect that keen avian eyesight has had on prey populations.

off a milkweed plant, you immediately see a flood of white latex sap laced with these toxins, poisons designed to dissuade animals from grazing on the plants. The boldly banded yellow, white and black monarch larvae can store the toxic defensive compounds found in the milkweed without ill effect, and when they metamorphose, the toxins are distributed primarily in the wings. As a result, an attack on a monarch by an unwitting bird is greeted with a nauseating smell. If the poisonous monarch is swallowed, the bird retches violently and thereafter avoids all monarchs.

By allowing young blue jays to eat either milkweed-reared monarchs or those reared on a nontoxic diet, the Browers showed that the association was learned. Birds that sampled the nontoxic monarchs ate them again and again without hesitation, while those that ate toxic butterflies learned to avoid them.

In nature, however, most monarchs are distasteful and avoided by birds. This presents other butterflies with a great evolutionary opportunity. Viceroy butterflies exploit the fact that black and orange monarch butterflies are nauseating. Viceroys feed on plants such as willow and are themselves palatable. Naïve blue jays eat them without hesitation, but the ones that have tasted a monarch avoid viceroys just as though they were monarchs. Because of their resemblance to monarchs, viceroys are protected from bird predation, and they gain this protection at the expense of the monarchs. If a bird first feeds on a viceroy, it will not hesitate to attack a monarch, perhaps damaging itself fatally in the learning process. Nevertheless, monarchs are so common that more birds learn to avoid their image than learn to like it because of an initial contact with a viceroy.

The avoidance image of the monarch must be forged anew in the mind of every young bird, and the viceroy's biology seems to take advantage of the timing of this learning. In Ontario, at least, the viceroy overwinters as a mature caterpillar, rolled up in a leaf bound by its silk to a branch. When it emerges as an adult in spring, it is first exposed only to old, experienced birds that have already learned about monarchs in previous summers. Later in the season, when migrating monarchs have returned to the north, nestling birds fledge and begin to feed, contacting a new generation of monarchs, which they quickly learn to avoid. Only later in summer does a second generation of viceroys emerge, ready to take advantage of the repellent image the monarchs have imprinted on a new generation of birds.

By the end of summer, the northern monarch population has grown large, and each butterfly faces the 2,000-mile voyage south to its overwintering sites in Mexico. In late September, I often sit by a large field overgrown with milkweed, purple asters and goldenrod, while hundreds of monarchs mass about me on the flowers. They sail off on their long trip south, protected by their bold orange and black patterns—letters of safe passage also imprinted in the minds of the millions of birds that will watch them travelling on.

Such systems of models and mimics are unstable defences that can become unbalanced should the mimic species become more abundant than the original image species. If the monarch's small southern range in Mexico suffers deforestation, effectively pushing the monarch to extinction, the demise of the viceroy could follow. The bold image they evolved could speed their end, attracting rather than repulsing predators. Evolution would favour viceroys whose appearance or behaviour could mimic another repugnant species.

But some models never change and are always available for mimicking. Many species of insects, rather than looking like something lethal or well defended, simply camouflage themselves as the perpetually abundant leaves, twigs, moss and lichens of the wild. Some of the mimics, like katydids, have not only the colour and form of dead leaves but also the veins, the chewed insect holes and spots of fungus all beautifully painted in place. There is a good reason for the exquisite craftsmanship. Because birds have nothing to fear from leaves and moss, they can search more carefully than when confronting more threatening items. Thus the insect must be superbly camouflaged to avoid detection.

Search Image

The discriminatory power of a bird's eye, coupled with avian learning ability, has produced some sophisticated insect camouflage techniques. Bernd Heinrich did an ingenious study of the prey-finding acumen of black-capped chickadees. He was moved to do the study when watching the curious behaviour of an underwing moth caterpillar feeding on basswood leaves. After eating for about an hour, the caterpillar left the half-eaten leaf to resume its resting place on a branch. However, before leaving the site of its meal, it spent five minutes laboriously chewing through the tough leaf stem and amputating the half-eaten leaf. Heinrich reasoned that the caterpillar was covering its tracks, getting rid of the damaged leaf that might alert birds to its presence.

Heinrich then conducted a simple experiment to see whether graduate students could also learn to use leaf damage as an indicator of caterpillar presence. All of the students learned to search more closely when they noticed chewed leaves and were able to locate more caterpillars. One student, finding that some caterpillars hid in rolled leaves, used leaf rolls as a cue. Another discovered that certain species of plants were heavily infested and selectively searched those bushes. Heinrich and a student then built an aviary and allowed captive chickadees to forage on different species of trees. Caterpillar density on the trees was controlled, and damaged leaves were either removed or simulated by clipping them with a paper punch. The chickadees proved to be astute searchers, able to use information about plant damage and identity. Heinrich concluded: "After many felled trees, some calluses and a daily dose of blackfly bites, we had found that the chickadees could use just about the same cues that graduate students do, but with more skill."

However, bird search images are also very inflexible. Alan Kamil and his coworkers at the University of Massachusetts have demonstrated that blue jays use very specific cues to build a search image, a sort of mental image which increases their ability to detect hidden prey. They trained caged blue jays to recognize images of a species of underwing moth sitting on bark. Photographs of just the bark alone or bark with a moth resting on it were projected on the cage wall, and the jays were allowed to peck at the image. Correct choices were rewarded with a food item. The birds readily learned to detect the moths and increased their skill as they gained experience.

What was remarkable about the experiment was that the birds did not generalize the image to include other species of underwing moths, even though they look rather similar when sitting at rest. When two species were presented, the jays showed no increased ability to detect the moths. In other words, the blue jays formed a highly specific search image for just one moth species at a time. They could not develop a search image that allowed them to increase detection of two species at once.

This has interesting implications for the explanation of why organisms look the way they do. Being odd can be highly adaptive if it places the individual outside common search images. Perhaps this is one reason why so much individual variation in appearance exists in certain insects, snails, frogs and even seed coats. The acute search-imaging bird's eye may be principal architect and judge of the appearance of insects, frogs, snakes, lizards, rodents, fruits—indeed, of anything that is food for birds.

As I walk through the forest, these questions occupy me: Does that boldly coloured beetle have a flavour which matches its pigments? Is the dark-patrolling nuthatch a connoisseur of lichen textures, able to discern the difference between the glint of a mottled moth and the dulled lustre of fungal fibre? And I understand that all we see around us are ancient, perpetually evolving images painted for other eyes.

INTELLIGENCE

The costs and benefits of having a brain

Late one August afternoon, I was paddling a dugout canoe along an oxbow lake in Amazonian Peru. The lake was bordered by a tangled wall of vines that hung from the treetops over the water. As I approached the green wall, I heard a strange sound, like heavy breathing. A hefty, ungainly bird, which looked like a cross between a chicken and a lizard, leapt from a branch and flapped awkwardly as it made a ponderous crash landing on the top of a fallen tree crown. I had seen my first hoatzin.

I laid up my paddle and stared. The bird had a glaring red eye highlighted by a surrounding patch of bare blue skin. A dishevelled crest of straggly feathers adorned its tiny head, and it used a long, wide tail to balance itself as it hopped about the tree crown. It was strangely reptilian; birds do not come any weirder than the hoatzin.

Among the hoatzin's more unusual features are its huge muscular crop and its wing claws, which enable its nestlings to negotiate vegetation. One of the few birds specialized for leaf eating, the hoatzin possesses a crop that occupies the upper third of its body, making it top-heavy, which, in combination with reduced flight muscles, explains the bird's awkward movement. While these characteristics account for much of the strangeness of the hoatzin, what struck me most was its air of primitive stupidity.

Every naturalist has observed that some birds behave more intelligently than others. People with bird feeders cannot help noticing the rapidity with which chickadees discover new food sources. Members of the crow family, especially ravens, are universally acclaimed for their intelligence, while other birds have come to symbolize stupidity. Europeans say someone is "as silly as a goose"; Australians use the expression "stupid as an emu"; North Americans speak of being "chicken-brained" and describe a fool as a "turkey."

These are more than anecdotal observations. Different species of birds show great variation in brain development. Some of the brainiest birds are crows, cockatoos, owls, woodpeckers and parrots. While unrelated

Hoatzins (left) are specialized leaf-eating cuckoos that live in South America. Most grazing birds appear to have lower brain weights than birds that hunt and eat a wide variety of prey.

Some foraging methods require sophisticated tactics. The group of white pelicans (above) has learned to fish as a team, herding minnows into the shallows where they can be caught. The emu (far right), a large grazing bird found in the dry open habitats of Australia, is considered by Australians to be the prototype of stupidity.

genetically, these birds each possess highly developed cerebral hemispheres and have a high brain-to-body weight ratio. The cerebellum is the area of the brain associated with learning and with integrating movement patterns. In the absence of any other objective measure, brain weight is a reasonable indicator of avian intelligence.

Studies of relative brain weight, incidentally, confirm one of my own prejudices about the intelligence of chickens: chickens and their relatives possess one of the smallest cerebellums of all birds. Emus, apparently, are first on the list, giving substance to the Australian expression.

Intelligence is notoriously difficult to define. Conventionally, it is equated with the ability to learn, a task that often requires a relatively large brain to store, organize and manipulate information. The many types of learning that animals are capable of make it problematic to attempt to measure avian intelligence with a single scale. The relative size of an animal's brain compared with its body weight is therefore simply a rough in-

dicator of the extent to which natural selection has favoured the animal's ability to deal with information.

Every trait, intelligence included, has costs associated with it. The brain is physiologically and energetically a very expensive organ to maintain. More than 20 percent of our own metabolism, for example, is devoted to fuelling the brain. Such a huge investment has to be justified by results. Unless increased intelligence pays off in increased reproductive success, less intelligent but more economically built birds will win the day because they will have the extra resources to devote to the demands of existence—reproduction, competition and predator avoidance. Learning ability is adjusted by natural selection to meet a specific set of ecological demands.

The relative size of a bird's brain seems to be less a consequence of its taxonomic group than of its life history. In other words, what a bird does determines how intelligent it has to be. I suspect that hoatzins are not intelligent because their simple feeding habits do not require that trait. While watching a hoatzin vacantly plucking at a vine tip, I recalled something evolutionary ecologist Phil Regal once told me about *Ameiva* lizards and the ecology of intelligence. Ameivas possess the highest brain-to-body weight ratio of all lizards, something that becomes apparent when one watches them feeding. Unlike many lizards that sit and wait, snapping passively at prey that happens by, ameivas busily seek out food, scuttling and rooting through the forest-floor litter, scaring up insects and unearthing larvae and pupae. Detecting and capturing a diverse range of prey is more demanding than nabbing a stationary item or stripping leaves from a branch.

Problem-Solving Intelligence

Ecological complexity lies at the heart of our question about why some birds are more intelligent than others. Twenty-five years ago, Peter Klopfer of Rockefeller University, in New York City, suggested that brain size correlates with ecological specialization and generalization, predicting that the brains of more specialized species would be smaller than those of generalists. Vegetarians require less intelligence than predators because plants are easy to harvest. Since the vegetarian hoatzin merely selects certain nutritious plant species, it has no need for the problem-solving intelligence required to capture and dispatch prey items under constantly changing conditions. Its foraging is simply pluck and grind.

The notion that a vegetarian diet is associated with lower avian intelligence has recently been supported by a survey of bird brain weights conducted by Peter Bennett of the University of Sussex and Paul Harvey of Oxford University. Reviewing patterns in brain weight in 139 species of birds in 54 families, Bennett and Harvey found that one of the few significant correlations was between large brain size and diet. Birds that preyed on a variety of lower vertebrates and invertebrates were substantially heavier-brained than vegetarians. Birds that pursued their prey through the forest canopy had relatively bigger brains than those

that pecked and browsed on the ground.

It follows that some birds may have evolved larger brains because they depend on complicated foraging methods. Great white pelicans, for example, often spread out in a line together and herd schools of fish into shallow bays where they can capture them easily. As an example of the extreme skill that some cooperatively foraging birds use, consider the account of toucan foraging

by David Mindell and Hal Black of Brigham Young University, in Utah. While on Barro Colorado Island in Panama, they witnessed a pair of chestnut-mandibled toucans pursuing a lizard. One of the toucans flew from its perch and hovered at the tree trunk where the lizard was hiding. The second toucan flushed it out, whereupon the lizard ran down the trunk and hid behind a philodendron leaf. Both toucans then perched closer to the tree. One rushed at the lizard, which scurried to the opposite side of the tree trunk where the other toucan was waiting. It caught the lizard in its bill and flew up to a branch, while the first toucan perched nearby. The toucan with the lizard bludgeoned it against the limb until its tail fell off. The other toucan swooped down and grabbed the tail, then the pair flew off together, having participated in a foraging feat that required considerable mental flexibility.

Behavioural Flexibility

A bird with the capacity to learn can customize its behaviour to suit local situations. I have watched oystercatchers along rocky Pacific coastlines using just such a learned ecological strategy. The oystercatcher has a long, sharply pointed, chisel-shaped bill that is neatly squared off at the tip—just like an oyster knife. The bill can be used to pry limpets and shellfish loose or to probe deep into beach sediments for soft prey. Young oystercatchers learn how to open mussels by watching their parents, which, interestingly, use one of two very different techniques to breach a mussel's tough bivalve shell. One technique is to carry the shellfish to a rock or some other firm substrate and hammer the mussel open at the weak point on the ventral side of the shell. The other method is to attack the mussel when it is slightly submerged and feeding. The oystercatcher drives its bill in through the siphon and slices the adductor muscles that hold the shell closed.

The method a nestling eventually adopts is determined entirely by the technique favoured by its parents. Stabbing is more profitable in areas where large mussels abound, whereas hammering is more effective with medium-sized mussels. If parents nest in areas where the mussel size matches their technique, their young will learn the appropriate method for the region. If mussels were all the same size, oystercatchers might have evolved a single set of instinctive motor patterns needed to open them. But mussels come in many sizes, and by learning a method from its experienced

parents, an oystercatcher can fine-tune its behaviour to the particular situation.

Russell Greenberg of the Smithsonian Institution has looked at the link between the food-finding behaviour of two different sparrow species and their behavioural flexibility. He compared neophobia—the fear of new things—in swamp and song sparrows. The swamp sparrow is ecologically specialized and rarely nests outside its marshy habitat. Song sparrows, on the other hand, will nest in a wide range of habitats and readily colonize areas opened by human disturbance. Greenberg set out feeding trays for the two species and filled them with brightly coloured man-made objects that neither sparrow could have previously experienced. The swamp sparrows were conservative and inhibited by the novel items, reducing their feeding rates by 60 percent

as a result of their phobia. By contrast, the ecologically flexible song sparrows continued to feed in the presence of the novelties, apparently unconcerned.

Because it lives in so many habitats, the song sparrow encounters a greater variety of unfamiliar objects in its daily life than does a swamp sparrow; this is reflected in the relative ease with which the song sparrow accepts the presence of novel items. The characteristic gives rise to the question, Does the song sparrow flourish in a wide range of habitats as a result of its mental flexibility, or does it possess this flexibility as a consequence of its habitat? In all likelihood, the two characteristics evolved in concert.

Feeding ecology, of course, is not the only determinant of relative intelligence. Long-lived birds, such as parrots, crows, jays and

woodpeckers, often have complicated social systems. The complexity of their social lives may be as important as their foraging ecology in determining relative brain size. Birds that travel in flocks, for example, can profit from observational learning. Naïve chickadees and other kinds of tits can learn to find, handle and eat new types of food by watching more experienced flock members. When a few English tits figured out how to open the lids of milk bottles sitting on doorsteps, the practice was rapidly copied until virtually all tits could perform the task. Less social birds such as raptors would have less to gain from possessing a brain capable of such a learning feat. Indeed, studies show that most raptors use largely instinctive reactions to recognize and secure their food.

The aptitude for learning a particular task, then, is very much determined by the ecology of the bird involved. Animal psychologist Marian Breland points out that a chicken can learn a visual task such as picking out a certain playing card marked with a small black dot from among a group of five different cards. A macaw has a difficult time performing such a feat, even though its larger brain and the development of its cerebellum indicate a greater learning ability than that of a chicken. Breland has shown that the ability of the macaw to learn the task depends on how the cards are marked. If the cards are coded with an indentation that the macaw can feel with its tongue, rather than recognize visually with a dot, the macaw easily discriminates between the cards. This makes sense, since macaws in the wild use their tongues and beaks constantly to open and process a tremendous variety of complex nuts and fruits.

While some birds forage instinctively, other species learn their hunting methods. The black oystercatcher (left) uses its specialized bill to pry off and open a variety of shellfish. Different types of shellfish require different capture and handling techniques. Oystercatchers learn particular methods and prey preferences by observing their parents. The swamp sparrow (above) prefers a narrow range of habitats and is less flexible in its behaviour than more generalist sparrows, such as the song sparrow. The ecological generalist must react to and interpret a greater variety of objects and events than birds with more restricted life histories. That may require a larger brain size.

Members of the parrot family, such as the scarlet macaw (above), are known to have relatively large brains in keeping with their complex vocalizations, a higher degree of sociality and a diet of great ecological complexity. The Laysan albatross (left) dutifully incubates a fishnet buoy that it has mistaken for an egg. In the albatross's natural environment, objects with this appearance are usually eggs, and the Laysan albatross has consequently evolved instinctive egg-recognition reactions. These responses are efficient under normal conditions, but a bird confronted by novel objects or circumstances can be easily misled.

Another example of the link between learning aptitude and ecology comes from the work of Alan Kamil of the University of Massachusetts. Kamil studied the spatial memory – or the ability to remember locations – of several different bird species that store food in caches. Various jays and other bird species hide nuts in the soil or on tree limbs and return to the sites after periods of time ranging from hours to a few months.

Efficient Responses

It is important to consider the natural context in which a behaviour occurs if we are to understand the value of learning or why some birds rely more on instinct than on learning. West German ethologist Eberhard Curio demonstrated that birds in the laboratory can be trained to fear and mob completely harmless objects. Between two cages containing blackbirds situated on opposite sides of a hallway, Curio placed a four-compartment box designed so that the blackbirds could see a stuffed bird in the compartment in front of them. They could not see what the neighbouring blackbirds were looking at but could hear their mobbing calls. Curio put blackbirds in two adjacent compartments. Opposite one group, he placed an owl, a natural enemy that blackbirds readily mob. Opposite another cage of blackbirds, he put an Australian honey guide, a bird the blackbirds never encounter and one that is not a standard object of mobbing attacks. The blackbirds opposite the owl became frenzied, calling and trying to mob it, just as they would in nature. That led the adjacent blackbirds to imitate the mobbing behaviour and to try to attack the harmless honey guide.

Removing the blackbirds that had learned to mob honey guides, Curio found he could use them to teach a totally naïve group of blackbirds to copy their behaviour. Using the same technique, he could even teach blackbirds to attack objects such as bottles. All that was necessary was a single exposure of the naïve birds to the mobbing calls of birds that seemed to be attacking the bottle.

While that particular experiment tends to make blackbirds seem foolish, their apparent foolishness is solely a result of the artificiality of the situation in which they were placed. We have all seen or heard of the stupidity of some birds — geese that adopt golf balls, robins that attack red-and-brown socks. As a result, we have a kind of disdain for instinctive behaviour. As naturalist Charlton Ogburn notes, "It is hard not to feel contempt for the budgerigar that snuggles up to a mirror."

The natural world, however, lacks vertical mirrors, and the budgie is not designed to account for their properties. In nature, likewise, there are few white spheres and ovoids, so it makes evolutionary sense for geese to have an efficient response to egglike objects because, in all probability, they *are* eggs. So, too, the robin attacking the crude model would normally be throttling a red-breasted male rival; we would not expect such a response to evolve if apples ripened and turned red in May. Instead of constituting a measure of idiocy, such reactions tell the naturalist what information is important and predictable in a bird's life.

Avian Personality

British ornithologist R.M. Lockley, author of *Puffins*, describes how easy it is to catch a puffin using a bamboo pole and a noose. The pole is inched slowly toward the puffin, which watches but does not move. The noose is slipped around its foot, and *voilà!* the puffin is caught. Lockley points out that the people of Scotland's St. Kilda Island noosed hundreds of puffins per person daily using this method. "You may decide from his behaviour that the puffin is stupid," writes Lockley. "And looking at him closely, you begin to see that the bird really resembles a clown. Apparently, he is not only mentally stupid, but he actually dresses like a clown, even to the false eyebrows, cheek smears and big, red, false-looking nose."

But as Lockley points out, puffins nesting on isolated cliffs have never had a reason to evolve a fear of bamboo rods and people. What we perceive as apparent stupidity is simply a bird placed in a situation for which its brain is not adapted. The natural economy does not confer intelligence that is not adaptively necessary.

The perspective allows us to appreciate the hoatzin in its proper context. As psychologist Breland put it, "Every animal is the smartest for the ecological niche in which it lives — if it were not, it would not be there."

The objective data to support this claim still do not exist; many a dedicated life would be taken up with the task of accumulating them. But enough is known to convince me that our anecdotal impressions of avian intelligence have real foundation and that we can look forward to the day when these impressions give way to a far larger, more complete science of avian personality. The thing we call personality is an amalgam of which intelligence is simply one aspect. The way a bird vocalizes, the tempo of its actions, the ease with which it can be approached, its tolerance for the presence of other birds — all these things are what give each group of birds, be they penguins, parrots or peewees, its unique personality.

Observers of wildlife are cautioned against overinterpreting and speculating about the meaning of animal behaviour in the absence of scientific data. Yet we must not be too inhibited. It will be a long while before we have scientific explanations for the intelligence and personality of birds. Until then, it is worth remembering that the wonderfully rich differences in avian personality we perceive are probably adaptations of consequence and meaning. Just as the vacant stare of the hoatzin speaks to me of its easy diet, I believe the quick, quirky personality of the warbler contains a similarly eloquent statement about its vulnerability to predators. The character of a raptor species willing and able to kill a mink is, with reason, fiercer than that of the raptors that eat insects. And the ponderous calm and seemingly wise aspect of the large forest owl is an attitude in keeping with the slow, sedentary pace of its long life and its need to be aware of each perch and tiny sound in its dark haunt.

IGNOBLE NATURE

Infanticide, cuckoldry and other natural acts

Each spring, a pair of phoebes builds a nest on the eaves of our house. They are gentle and mild-mannered, working together and quietly raising one or two sets of nestlings. Sitting on the telephone line, calmly flipping their tails or occasionally dropping down to pluck a caterpillar from the garden, they seem like exemplary additions to the household.

Who would suspect that these placid birds have a darker side? Consider an observation reported in an ornithological paper: A female phoebe in search of a nest viciously pecked at a clutch of phoebe nestlings until she succeeded in throwing them out of their nest. The male parent fluttered about helplessly, trying to feed the dying nestlings. Meanwhile, the female had begun to perform courtship solicitation displays on the nest. The male, recognizing defeat, surrendered and eventually mated with her. A week after the liquidation of the male's first offspring, the pair initiated its own clutch of nestlings.

How does the naturalist make sense of such behaviour? Frank Chapman, one of the century's most widely read ornithologists and the author of the authoritative text *Bird Life*, suggests to his readers that "if you would reap the purest pleasures of youth, manhood and old age, go to the birds and through them be brought within the ennobling influences in nature." The idea of a benign and forgiving natural world is indeed an appealing one; yet those who actually go out and observe nature soon discover that it is far from gentle.

The intentional destruction of eggs and nestlings occurs in a variety of birds, including acorn woodpeckers, purple martins, scrub jays, house wrens and tree swallows, and it can be perpetrated by either the male or the female. There are incidents so bizarre that it appears the bird has become unhinged. In one case, a female tree swallow invaded five different nest boxes over a two-week period, killing a total of 25 nestlings. Patricia Gowaty of Clemson University, in South Carolina, has documented the conflict between female bluebirds, which

These male prairie chickens (left) are fighting in earnest. In an attempt to increase their own reproductive success, birds, like other organisms, often damage members of their own species.

113

Nestling gulls (above) frequently peck their brothers or sisters to drive them away from the nest. Siblicide is a common occurrence in a variety of seabirds, raptors and songbirds. The little blue heron (far right) has just pushed its sibling off its perch while the mother stood passively by. Parental birds do not normally interfere with sibling rivalry, even though it can lead to the death of some of their offspring.

battle over nest sites, surreptitiously dumping eggs into other females' nests and sometimes even murdering one another.

Moralists explain nature's violence by arguing that individual suffering is demanded by the higher purpose of maintaining a balanced ecosystem. A classic example of such rationalization is that predators cull the sick and old members of a species and thereby benefit the prey population. Of this, 19th-century philosopher Arthur Schopenhauer observed that the pain of natural functions is outweighed, or at least balanced, by the pleasure, and he urged, "If the reader wishes to see shortly whether this statement is true, let him compare the respective feelings of two animals, one of which is engaged in eating the other."

Melancholy Reflection

The belief that individuals are sacrificed for a greater good—the good of the species— is time-honoured. Thomas Bewick, an 18th-century British authority on birds, accounted for the carnage thusly: "It is a melancholy reflection that from man downwards to the smallest living creature, all are found to prey upon and devour each other. The philosophic mind, however, sees this waste of animal life again and again repaired by fresh stores, ever ready to supply the void, and the great work of generation and destruction perpetually going on and, to this dispensation of an all-wise Providence, so interesting to humanity, bows in awful silence." Such sentiments persist throughout the writings of many naturalists. For a time, it was common for famous ethologists such as Konrad Lorenz and Eibl-Eibesfeldt to condemn the notion of "nature red in tooth and claw" as a misguided view of life. They interpreted much of what they saw as adaptations designed to protect the species, even at the expense of the individual.

As evolutionary biologist Richard Dawkins puts it, these authors "got it totally and utterly wrong. . . . I think 'nature red in tooth and claw' sums up our modern understanding of natural selection quite admirably." What we actually see in nature are *individuals* striving to perpetuate the genes that constitute them. The focus of natural selection is on the individual, the real entity directly involved in the transmission and replication of its genes. That realization has had a strong impact on the way birds are studied.

Raleigh Robertson of Queen's University at Kingston, Ontario, gives us an example of how the approach is practised. In Robertson's study of the adaptive significance of infanticide in tree swallows, the focus is on individual birds. Each breeding unit is captured and marked with distinctive coloured leg bands. Its behaviour and reproductive success are then followed throughout the breeding season. In hayfields outfitted with nest boxes that allow for easy capture, marking and observation of the birds, the reproductive success of each bird can be tabulated. Sometimes, marked birds return over successive seasons, which allows for a long-term accumulation of information on individuals. The close scrutiny of the fates of individuals, rather than the species or population as a whole, has shown in detail how individuals struggle and risk death to win in their competition with others for food, nest sites and mates.

When he experimentally removed males, Robertson found that a replacement male soon took over the nest box. The replacement often killed the nestlings and then quickly renested with the female, which promptly laid another clutch of eggs. If the female left the territory, the replacement male lost little time attracting another mate. In this study, infanticide clearly seems to be the result of the severe competition for nest sites and the existence of a large "floater" population of unpaired males and females. The logic of infanticide lies in the limited supply of boxes, mates and breeding opportunities. The extremely infanticidal swallow female mentioned earlier was unpaired and faced possible genetic extinction unless she could disrupt a breeding pair and replace another female. The infanticidal males in Robertson's study increased their reproductive success by removing competitors' offspring and replacing them with their own. Indeed, in all of the many cases of infanticide documented, the motivation appears to have been genetic self-interest. The infanticidal individual stood to gain in terms of increased reproductive success.

Perpetuation of the species is not the driving force of evolution but is merely the consequence of the more fundamental force of natural selection, which favours genetic traits that enhance the reproductive success of the individuals which carry them. In fact, the selection for individuals that do their utmost to reproduce as much as possible often works against the perpetuation of the species through overpopulation and degradation of the environment.

When this approach to bird behaviour is applied, the ruthless genetic struggle shows up even in species that appear to have a cooperative social system. In Costa Rica, I often spend time watching groove-billed anis. The chunky, black birds are so highly social that I cannot recall ever seeing one not in the close company of its peers. They sit amicably at the edges of fields, waiting for the horses or cattle to flush up insects. Once I stayed in a beach house that had a lemon tree beside the second-storey balcony. A group of anis began to construct a nest right beside my hammock. The nest building was a joint venture with about half a dozen birds collectively searching for twigs and weaving them into a large communal nest. These fragments of ani life might have made me conclude that the species, at least, is free from selfish strife. But when Sandra Vehrencamp of the University of California took a detailed look at ani individuals, she found the same strain of genetic competition with which we are now acquainted interwoven in their cooperative breeding system. It merely took another form.

The female anis rolled each other's eggs out of the nest, thereby destroying them. The outcome of that contest was based on a female dominance hierarchy. Subdominant females laid their eggs earliest, and the dominant female laid her eggs last. Apparently, females cannot distinguish their eggs from those of others, so they roll eggs before they begin laying and then cease. The last female to lay her eggs succeeds in

leaving the largest number of offspring. More important, although females nest communally, they continue to try to better one another reproductively.

The perception of nature as being informed by violence is a troubling one. Naturalist/writer Annie Dillard, in discussing the overproduction and relentless culling of individuals which occur in the natural world, concluded that "either this world, my mother, is a monster, or I myself am a freak." Dillard's value system could not account for the fact that organisms are selected not to produce the number of offspring that stabilizes the population but the number that maximizes their descendants, which means individuals usually produce more offspring than can survive.

The instance of excess fecundity that has most affected me did not involve large num-

115

bers. I was in southern Saskatchewan, an eroded rolling landscape of shortgrass prairie and clay bluffs. From the top of one bluff, I could look down into a golden eagle's nest just a few yards below. A large, fluffy white chick perched contentedly on the massive platform of sticks surrounded by an assortment of jackrabbit legs and portions of ground squirrels. It looked as though the hunting was good and the living easy. But below the nest on the ground was another snow-white figure. I scrambled down the bluff for a look and found a large, well-formed eagle nestling lying on the clay, having evidently fallen to its death. It seemed a tragedy to me that a nestling already well along the road to becoming a rare and great raptor should have been purposely destroyed. But I knew there was nothing amiss here. It is routine for one golden eagle nestling to harass and finally push its younger sibling to its death. Golden eagles always lay two eggs, and the second nestling to hatch is killed by the first.

Many raptors lay two eggs but rear only one offspring. It is common for other birds to lay a larger clutch than they can rear. In a good year, most nestlings may fledge, but in a bad year, several nestlings may starve or be driven out of the nest. This reproductive strategy is known to ornithologists, somewhat euphemistically, as "brood reduction." It is characteristic of many bird species, seabirds and raptors in particular, but is also seen in species as different as sparrows, snow buntings and white pelicans.

Ecologists debate the reasons why some birds have obligatory brood reduction while others practise optional brood reduction and some do not seem to exhibit any brood reduction at all. There is a variety of explanations, such as the availability and predictability of food resources, whether or not the birds nest in cavities and the likelihood of infertile or damaged eggs. The literature on the topic is vast. But regardless of the specific ecological explanation of brood reduction, the driving evolutionary force remains the same: brood reduction occurs because it raises the reproductive success of the parents.

The treatment that parents mete out to their nestlings is often not in the direct interest of the nestlings. Gulls that hatch two or three chicks may not feed the third chick enough for it to survive. Parental reproductive success is maximized by the production of one or two vigorous fledglings rather than three weaker offspring. The third nestling, of course, should not stoically comply with this arrangement. Natural selection favours individuals that do all they can to survive and reproduce despite parental neglect and sibling competition.

Predictions of behaviour that are based on natural selection have borne some unusual fruit by making sense of the phenomenon of adoption among colonial seabirds. It has been shown that in colonial gull species such as kittiwakes, the expendable last-hatched offspring often leaves its nest and ingratiates itself with another pair of adults within the nesting territory. The chick may move to a new nest with smaller offspring, kill or displace the younger chicks and pass itself off as the legitimate offspring.

The trumpeter swan (above) is aggressively chasing Canada geese away from its cygnets. Some species of waterfowl and seabirds will peck and kill the unattended young of others. The fighting Canada geese (top right) exhibit in their aggression the fundamentally competitive nature of natural selection. Behaviours evolve when they enhance the success of one individual over other members of the species. The aggression displayed by nesting royal terns (right) is an adaptation an individual uses to increase its ability to gain resources, such as space, that contribute to its reproductive success.

Kittiwake nestlings will push eggs or small chicks off the cliff ledge to create an opportunity for themselves. Adoption in this case amounts to the chick's parasitism of the parental care of genetically unrelated adults. The risk of such parasitism is one reason that colonial seabird adults often attack and kill wandering chicks which approach their nesting territory.

Genetic Competition

Some naturalists may feel that the actual mechanism of evolution has little to do with their perception of nature. After all, evolution is an almost imperceptibly slow process when measured against the rapid pace of our brief lives. But most of what we experience in nature is anecdotal—we cannot stop and experimentally test the meaning of our observations— and as a result, our beliefs determine our experience of natural history. I recall an incident involving two scarlet-thighed dacnis males in Costa Rica. They were fluttering beside one another on the ground, so engrossed in each other that I was able to stand right beside them. The sunlight played on their plumage; flitting back and forth at each other, they looked almost like courting iridescent blue morpho butterflies. It would have been easy for me to imagine they were playing or participating in a harmless ritual. How often have we read that aggression is ritualized so as to prevent injury to the combatants? But thinking selectively made me believe that what I saw was not play or ritual but two dacnis males fighting a territorial battle, engaged in an issue of genetic competition so earnest that they were blind to my threat. Right before my eyes, those two beautiful beings were trying to annihilate each other.

When I was digging among ornithology texts in the basement of the university library, a file card slipped out of one of the books. On the card were the notes of a schoolteacher who had gone to the library to prepare a lesson on birds for a grade-three class. The teacher had listed the following items as the basis of the lesson: birds building a nest; mother keeping eggs warm; eggs hatching; mother and father going out, taking turns to find food; baby birds being fed; baby birds learning to fly; birds resting quietly in the nest. How pleasant was the domestic scene set by the teacher! Too pleasant, I suspect, for the distressing concept of brood reduction.

Humans are often reluctant to acknowledge the harshness of the natural world. But that willingness to obscure reality is the very reason the logic of natural selection is so essential to the naturalist. To impose human moral standards of behaviour thoughtlessly upon other species is inappropriate at best and, at worst, dangerous; to pretend that as observers of the natural world, we are capable of neutral objectivity is just as perilous. British biologist D.R. Crocker argues that we should confront the inherent anthropomorphism which colours our contemplation of animal behaviour. "It is an imperative self-discipline to try and weed out what you saw happen from what you think it meant," he writes. "However, meaning is where the meat is. . . . Our understanding of ourselves and our societies is the material we inevitably use to build theories of animal social behaviour. We should not cover it up." Indeed, much of what goes on in nature is so distasteful to conventional human morality that thinking selectively is the only way we become aware of many phenomena. The price we pay is that we see things much more bleakly once the logic of natural selection becomes part of our world view.

Darwin saw both the dark and the bright side of this perspective. He exclaimed in a letter to a colleague: "What book a devil's chaplain might write on the clumsy, wasteful, blundering, low and horribly cruel works of nature!" Yet in the last paragraph of *The Origin of Species*, he concludes: "There is grandeur in this view of life." He recognized that "from the war of nature, from famine and death, the most exalted object which we are capable of conceiving, namely, the production of the higher animals, directly follows."

The degree of this exaltation is not easy

to grasp. Without some measure, it is hard to determine just how finely honed all individuals are when in their natural state. But look at a domesticated turkey bred for a cloistered life within the confines of a poultry factory. I chased some domesticated turkeys down inside a barn in preparation for Thanksgiving dinner one year. They were huge, meaty birds, but with their vacuous stupidity and their monotonous white plumage, they were sad shadows of the wily wild tom, with his flaring tail fan of shining blacks and rich chestnuts.

Almost no concoction bred by humans in a laboratory has ever been able to survive when released into the natural world. The wild type prevails, and that is a measure of the yield of natural selection. We cannot condemn natural selection and its attendant horrors for this very reason: there is not one wild bird that is less than wonderful. Why is that? It is because each individual that lives has been selected and culled, tested and tried—again and again and again. That process can be horrifying, but it has this reward: all those which remain here with us possess, out of that enduring contest, the incredibly exacted form and vitality of survivors.

Situations in which natural selection has been relaxed or altered by domestication produce birds such as these turkeys (far left) that have been selected for their passive tolerance of captivity under crowded conditions. The result is an uncompetitive bird unable to survive the rigours of the natural environment or competition from wild birds. By contrast, the magnificently plumaged wild tom turkeys fighting during breeding season (above) display the impressive consequences of countless generations of selection for survival and reproductive traits.

RELATIONSHIPS
Odd couplings and the politics of parasitism

On the road to town, there is a large, dying oak at the beginning of a sharp curve, a bend that I often negotiate with too much haste. But a scene in the oak tree sometimes makes me check my pace. Turkey vultures perch there, sunning their bellies, erect on the bare oak limbs in the early-morning light. They stand there with their huge wings spread and their long pinion feathers fanned, an eerie reminder of mortality.

Turkey vultures are recent additions to the fauna of eastern Ontario, having bred in this vicinity only within the last 15 years. Their expansion corresponds to the increase in road kills and, possibly, the decimation of the wolf population. In any case, turkey vultures are now here in force, processing woodland and roadside carrion into nutrition for the living.

Not everyone applauds the arrival of these birds; the scavenging habits of vultures tend to horrify people. I admit it is a macabre experience to round a bend in the road and suddenly encounter vultures leaping up from a freshly mangled raccoon like huge,

Turkey vultures (left), here poised to catch the early-morning sun, have been reviled and praised by various observers because of their taste for carrion.

black, gore-spattered phantoms. My neighbours find their bald heads and long necks ugly. Perhaps there are unpleasant connotations to the possible adaptive function of the vulture's bare pate. One anonymous 18th-century English writer on vultures graphically expressed his view on the subject: "It is often their custom, when glutting on their foul repast, to bury head and neck in the eagerness of the moment in the putrescent mass, so that were these parts covered with feathers, the utmost inconvenience would arise from their being saturated with gore and filth and drying into a hardened, clotted layer."

But even those who are repelled by the vulture's eating habits must concede its usefulness. One of my older natural-history books unabashedly describes the vulture as "cowardly, filthy and voracious." But the author goes on to point out that in the Tropics, vultures provide an "infinite service to the inhabitants by devouring that filth which otherwise, by its intolerable stench, would render the climate still more unwholesome

121

Many naturalists will counter that there are plenty of tasks in nature, such as pollination and seed dispersal, which require what some ecologists refer to as mutualism (a relationship beneficial to both participants) and which bind different species together in interdependency. Medical researcher, physician and best-selling author Lewis Thomas is one of many proponents of this view. In *Lives of a Cell*, he writes: "Most of the associations between living things we know about are essentially cooperative ones, symbiotic to one degree or another. . . . Every creature is, in some sense, connected to and dependent on the rest."

My old natural-history book expressed it this way: "All things which do exist owe such existence to their compatibility with other existences; to the necessary fitness of all existing things; and to the harmony essential to the existence of anything in the form and mode in which it does exist." In pre-Darwinian times, the relationship between physical form and function was often used to prove the existence of a divine designer.

The turkey vulture is superbly adapted for scavenging. Its sense of smell allows it to forage for carrion in woodland. Odour trails guide it to carcasses hidden in deep forest and even buried under brush piles. Its digestive system is, needless to say, incredibly resistant to bacterial contaminants and toxins. It can eat anthrax and cholera bacteria with impunity. A dose of botulism toxin that would destroy a village of people has absolutely no effect on the turkey vulture. Looking at the vulture this way makes it seem that there is indeed a sense of harmony "in the form and mode in which it does exist."

There is some sense to the forms of things and to the relationships among them. But what do the patterns really mean in terms of essential ecological integrity? I think of the ruby-throated hummingbirds hovering at the cardinal flowers in our garden. When I sit under a blue summer sky and watch the ruby-throats probing the spikes of crimson in a blur of iridescent light and see the white pollen dusted above their bills, the sheer beauty of the sight suggests the rightness

than it is." The author, a firm believer in divine creation, felt compelled to justify the existence of the loathsome vulture by identifying its useful ecological role in carrying out a task that benefits humanity. Around the world, laws have been passed to protect vultures from persecution because of the service they perform.

Such justification of a species has never been more prevalent than at present. As development continues to encroach on the natural world, naturalists and conservationists are continually called upon to answer the question, But what good is it? The naturalist generally answers that it is a useful scavenger or that it eats insects. But should we try to justify a creature by its alleged natural utility rather than by the attributes for which we really value it?

Ecologist Marston Bates has suggested that the best response the naturalist can give to this question is to ask, What good are *you*? Bates goes on to say that the question asked about species ought to be, What is its role in the economy of nature? A popular formula for justifying the existence of species other than our own has been to show how they make ecosystems work and to describe how species are bound together by a web of ecological relationships that create

a vital living fabric. "We rend this cloth at our peril" becomes the message that is drawn from such tightly bound relationships. Ecologists and conservationists in particular have often presented this argument for preserving species.

Yet the picture of the ecological world as a balanced, harmonious system built of cooperative or necessary relationships between species is simply not accurate. It dangerously oversimplifies the dynamic nature of ecological relationships. In truth, I have used this ploy myself, but I concede it is a dishonest means of achieving the justified end of species preservation.

In fact, many ecological relationships are neither obligatory nor essential for the survival of ecosystems. Turkey vultures, for example, are not indispensable components of the eastern deciduous forest. They may be useful scavengers, but if they did not exist, there are legions of other organisms, such as skunks, opossums, flies, beetles and microbes, that would readily scavenge the same carcasses. The relationship between turkey vultures and the rest of the natural world is asymmetrical: turkey vultures depend utterly on the world's carrion, but the natural world is not dependent on turkey vultures.

and necessity of the partnership between bird and flower.

Mutualistic Coevolution

The cardinal is a classic hummingbird flower. It has a long, bright red bloom that is easy for hummingbirds to see in the greenery along the lakeshores and stream-banks favoured by the plant. The narrow corolla is wide enough for the long tongue and bill of the hummer but narrow enough to exclude bees. It has no perfume to speak of, since birds only rarely use this cue to identify or find flowers. During the day, when the birds are active, the blossoms secrete large quantities of nectar, and their anthers protrude well out in order to daub pollen on the face of the hovering hummingbird.

For their part, the ruby-throats do a good job of pollinating; I always find well-set seed in the cardinal flowers I check. The plants tend to have a stretched-out distribution along a narrow strip of wetland. And the highly mobile hummer ensures a cardinal flower effective long-distance cross-pollination. All of these things considered, the relationship between the bird and the flower seems to be a neat example of mutualistic coevolution.

The beauty of their interaction also makes it easy to accept as proper and necessary. But the sight of a vulture raising its spattered hooked beak from the belly of a porcupine requires us to work at believing in the necessity of vultures; we are rarely forced to make such intellectual justifications for hummingbirds or flowers. That is a general problem for the naturalist: it is easy to be beguiled by the beauty of an ap-

These turkey vultures (far left) tuck into a meal of rabbit. The bird's head and neck are uniquely adapted to its feeding habits: free of feathers, the bird can explore messy carcasses without carrying away traces of the rotting flesh. The cattle egrets now common in cattle pastures in the Americas were once followers of African big game, like these Cape buffalo (above), which the egrets use as "beaters." As the herd advances, it stirs up insects that the egrets catch and eat. The egret's foraging success is greater when it follows a herd than when it searches by itself, but it appears to matter little what particular species of grazer it chooses to follow.

Although flowers that are specialized for humming-bird pollination tend to have tubular red and orange corollas, all hummingbirds, such as this female ruby-throated hummingbird (above), visit a wide variety of flowers. The pollen-bearing anthers of the red Columnea flowers growing on a Costa Rican mountainside are designed so that their pollen adheres to the forehead and bill of the male violet sabre-wing hummingbird (left). The oxpecker (far right) performs a mutually beneficial function by eating the insects that attack the African rhino.

parent match between form and function, to be lulled into believing that this is a harmonious relationship.

A closer look at the cardinal flower/hummingbird interaction, however, revealed that the relationship is much more subtle than previously suspected. Ecologists Jim and Astrid Kodrick Brown found a population of cardinal flowers that produced no nectar. The hummingbirds in this area were taking nectar from such flowers as the gilia. They also visited the nectarless cardinal flowers, possibly because they look like gilia flowers. The best interpretation of the situation is that these particular cardinal flowers are deceptive mimics of other species of red tubular flowers which do secrete nectar. They attract hummingbirds and are pollinated but provide no rewards for the birds. Plants like these cardinal flowers have clearly been designed by natural selection to maximize their reproductive success even if their design does not match the needs of hummingbirds.

The flower's evolutionary interest, then, does not have to match the hummingbird's needs. Bob Montgomerie of Queen's University at Kingston, Ontario, has shown that hummingbirds actually prefer flowers with a short corolla tube because they can extract nectar at an increased rate. Nectar deep down in a corolla takes more effort to remove. That ties in with a finding of Richard Miller of Yale University, who argues that hummingbird flowers are consistently designed to make hovering a necessity for hummingbirds despite the fact that hummingbirds are inclined to perch rather than hover. Miller demonstrated that given an opportunity to perch while feeding, hummers perch. Hovering is so energetically costly that the birds burn less energy if they sit while feeding.

The time a hummingbird spends visiting a plant will depend on how much nectar is in the flowers. It will remain at the plant only as long as the nectar yields exceed the costs of hovering, which means that a hovering bird moves on sooner and visits more plants than does a bird allowed to perch. If the hummer is allowed to perch, it can afford

to remain at a plant, draining each blossom of all its nectar. In other words, by evolving a form that forces hummingbirds to hover, the plant ensures that its pollen gets moved farther and to more target plants. The plant clearly has evolutionary interests that differ from those of the hummingbird. From the plant's perspective, the hummingbird is merely a resource that the plant exploits in order to enhance its own reproductive success.

When one looks again at the cardinal flower, the form of its flower appears not as evidence of a strong mutualistic relationship but as a means of excluding less effective pollinators. And look again at the hummingbird: its long bill is not designed to enable it to visit and pollinate these flowers but simply to allow it to outcompete others intent on gathering nectar.

Harmonious Interactions

Competition between species raises an even greater challenge to the notion that all species' interactions are necessary and harmonious. In Monteverde, Costa Rica, where I often spend the winter, there are some 22 hummingbird species pollinating more than 100 plant species. Many of the same plants are also pollinated by but-

terflies, moths and bees. Are all these hummingbird species necessary to the floral community?

Peter Feinsinger, an ecologist at the University of Florida who has studied this ecological community for many years, has shown that there are several generalist species visiting and competing for access to a mixture of short-corolla flowers. Feinsinger points out that the relationship between the flowers and the hummingbirds appears to be mutually beneficial. Competition among the different pollinators results in virtually every one of these kinds of flowers being visited. Yet, as Feinsinger emphasizes, "the community-level mutualism is a result, not a cause, of selection acting in each plant or animal population."

The distinction is important. It is easy to believe that such a community functions because of cooperative interactions. But a high pollination rate is a result of competition among hummingbirds. Under such conditions, the presence of any one hummingbird species is not essential; if a generalist hummingbird species were removed, the plants would still get pollinated.

Ecologist Paul Colinvaux in *Why Big Fierce Animals Are Rare* concluded that "peaceful coexistence, not struggle, is the

rule of our Darwinian world." Colinvaux claimed that his conclusion stands as "one of the most heartening lessons of biology." I cannot agree. Twenty-two hummingbird species coexist in the Monteverde area. If one puts up a feeder, it becomes a perpetual battleground, with hummingbirds diving and chasing their rivals. Anyone who has watched these hummingbirds could never subscribe to the idea that their coexistence

is peaceful. When the violet sabre-wing discovers the mountain gem at the feeder or flower patch, the mountain gem is driven off in an aggressive flurry.

To be fair to Colinvaux, he was indirectly arguing that species tend to evolve behaviours that enable them to survive competition from other species. He cited the famous study of warbler foraging by Robert Mac-Arthur, the Princeton ecologist who moved ecology ahead by a quantum leap in the 1960s and early 1970s. He found that different warblers could forage in the same spruce tree, some species consistently foraging lower down or farther out on the tree crown than others. In MacArthur's view, it was this subdivision of the resource that enabled the various species to coexist.

It sounds appealingly harmonious, but how is this separation maintained? Foraging

Many birds, including the goldfinch (left), are dependent on plants yet provide no mutual dispersal services. The goldfinch is simply a seed predator that destroys seeds when it eats them. Flicking a long tubular tongue out of its bill, the rufous hummingbird (above) is about to resume its nectar-gathering attack on a patch of spring blossoms. The hummingbird, possessing a wingspan of less than five inches, doggedly follows spring from Mexico to as far north as Alaska each year.

127

The ravens brazenly contriving to steal salmon from a distracted grizzly bear (above) are—along with various jays and gulls—notorious food thieves. Mixed flocks of birds composed of several different species, such as this group of egrets and gulls (right), often form temporarily. The interaction between these different species ranges from intense competition to benign indifference.

bird flocks are structured by aggressive dominance relationships. Remove one species from the mixed flock, and individuals of another soon begin to use the uncontested area. Natural selection favours individuals that exploit undefended opportunity. Anyone who feeds birds in the wintertime has seen firsthand how the jays dominate smaller birds, how the downies give way to the hairy woodpeckers and how the finches avoid the aggressive pecks of the nuthatches. The fact that individuals from one species compete with individuals from another contradicts the notion that each species plays a unique and irreplaceable role in the natural economy.

It would be wrong, however, to ignore the fact that there are highly evolved relationships between birds and other species which are mutualistic and virtually oblig-

atory. There are fruit-eating birds that seem to be tied to the parasitic mistletoe plants, and vice versa. In order for a mistletoe seedling to become established, it must land on a tree branch, which it accomplishes by attracting birds that eat its fruit and disperse the seed. Several specialized birds, like the mistletoe bird of Australia and the white-cheeked cotinga, depend almost entirely on mistletoe for food. The white-cheeked cotinga is even reported to wipe the masses of regurgitated seeds into likely germination spots on branches. Other birds, such as chlorophonias in Central America and phainopeplas in the United States, also eat large quantities of mistletoe fruits and are important dispersal agents.

Both the mistletoe and these birds have adaptive features related to their interaction. The mistletoe seed has a sticky coat of viscin

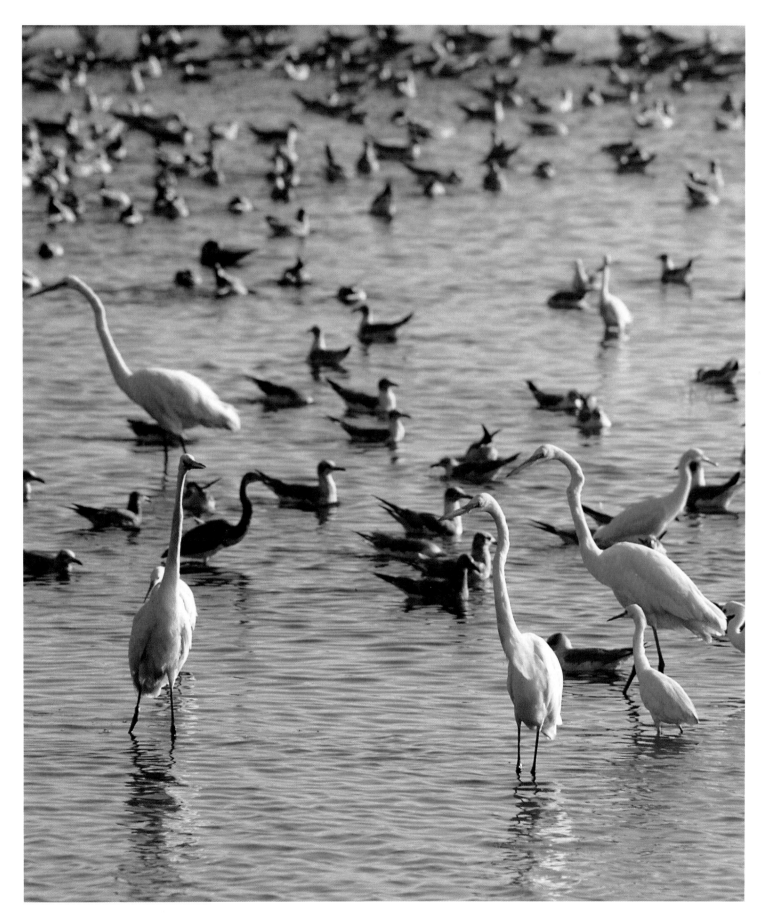

pointed out that "examples of this sort seem to please most people, perhaps because we find the thought of cooperation among humans an appealing idea, and its occurrence elsewhere suggests that harmony is a natural state of affairs, or at least a possible one."

Other plants, such as the tropical laurels, have made even greater commitments to the needs of their avian dispersers. Not only are the fruits large and conspicuously advertised with bold black, orange and red colours, but they are also more nutritious than the temperate fruits and berries. Wild avocados, for example, are tremendously rich in protein and oil, which enables bellbirds to raise their offspring on a diet of fruit. The birds do disperse some of the seeds, but I commonly see resplendent quetzals or bellbirds spit out seed after seed beside the tree from which the fruit was plucked. Such seeds are destined to die in the shade of their parent. If the bird does disperse the seed, it is because it has been forced to carry the fruit away to avoid exposure to predators or competitors. It is individual self-interest, rather than interspecies cooperation, that drives the system.

In western North America, Clark's nutcrackers and whitebark pines have a similar relationship. There is again evidence of coadaptation between the birds and the trees. The seeds of whitebark pines are heavy and lack wings for aerial dispersal. In fact, the cones remain closed until nutcrackers tear into them. The nutcrackers have a specialized long bill and a large mouth pouch that they use for harvesting and transporting seeds. The seed caches of the nutcrackers are often located in open areas far from the parental trees, and usually a surplus of seeds remains to germinate.

Studies of other birds and rodents seem to show that their foraging habits do not result in effective dispersal or germination. The relationship between the whitebarks and nutcrackers appears to be an obligatory mutualism. Without the nutcrackers, whitebark pines might die out; the nutcrackers would perhaps become extinct if the whitebark pines were removed. But it is worth

that anchors it to whatever surface it lands on. The mistletoe-feeding birds lack a tough gizzard and do not damage the seed; they either regurgitate it or pass it intact. Unspecialized birds, without the modified gizzard, would destroy the seed. But the seed is protected by toxins released when it is damaged, deterring birds that might act as both fruit eaters and seed predators.

In the southwestern United States, phain-

opeplas and mistletoe are closely bound. The phainopeplas use insects to feed their young, but they themselves eat hundreds of mistletoe berries daily. If the mistletoe crop fails, the phainopeplas will not breed. For their part, the birds evidently do a good job of dispersing the seeds. I have seen vast areas of Sonoran Desert in which every mesquite was festooned with mistletoe.

Behavioural ecologist John Alcock has

remembering that the origins of the relationship are rooted in simple seed predation. The plant merely compensates by producing a large surplus and relies on the inability of the birds to retrieve or use all of its seed hoards.

Mast Year

Dependence by a plant on its seed predator was first described in 1939 by ecologist Joseph Grinnel, who noted that oaks were incapable of dispersing uphill. After a fire or other form of deforestation, jays replanted the oaks by dispersing acorns to uphill areas.

The range of interactions between birds and plant seeds is a continuum: at one end are a few rare obligatory mutualists; at the other end is seed predation with no dispersal. Many bird/seed interactions fall into the latter category. The most spectacular of the predator/prey conflicts are the mass migrations of northern populations south of their usual range: the great grey and snowy owls come south when the northern rodent populations plunge; seed-eating birds such as crossbills, redpolls, grosbeaks, pine siskins and purple finches often pour into the south following a crop failure of conifer seeds.

Most northern trees have highly erratic seed-production schedules. Usually, all the trees in a large geographic area are reproductively synchronized by some weather-related cues. In a "mast year," the trees flower and generate a huge crop of seed, known as mast. The year of abundance is followed by a variable number of years in which no crop is produced. Unpredictable reproductive timing is adaptive for the trees because

Phainopeplas living in the southwestern United States cannot breed unless there is a large crop of mistletoe fruits. The bird (far left) cleans off and digests the outer coating of mistletoe, leaving the seed unharmed. When it visits the branches of a mesquite tree, it distributes the seeds, which then germinate and root as parasites on the mesquite. The northern mockingbird (above) defends winter territories that are rich in berries. All winter long, it feeds on the high-calorie fruits and disperses the seeds in the process.

The crossbill (above) is a seed predator that uses its curved bill to remove the seeds of the coniferous tree. Through its habit of seeding erratically and synchronizing production over huge areas, the tree subjects the crossbills to boom-and-bust episodes of abundance and scarcity. The tree's adaptation evolved to mitigate the effects of seed predation, and as a consequence, crossbills have been forced to migrate great and potentially dangerous distances when the crop fails. Central American birds, such as the resplendent quetzal (far right), also interact ecologically with plants. The quetzal has a tremendous gape and a modified stomach designed to allow the bird to feed on the fruits and disperse the large seeds of the wild avocado.

they swamp the seed-predator populations in mast years, and then, in succeeding years, the predators starve down to low population levels. By the time the next mast year occurs, few seed predators are alive. These vagaries in seed production cause mass starvation in organisms such as squirrels and seed-eating birds. They even force Clark's nutcrackers to migrate periodically in search of food. The migrations of boreal seed-eating birds are accompanied by a failure to breed.

It is clear that the value of birds as seed dispersers has not been sufficient to select for plants that consistently produce an abundance of seeds in order to support stable populations of their dispersers. In fact, the relationship between oaks and conifers and their seed dispersers is a system of mutual exploitation, rather than one of cooperation.

What is the thread connecting these observations: competition between hummingbird species, mimicry by cardinal flowers, mast-seeding that decimates dispersers? It is the individual self-interest favoured by natural selection that drives all these systems and generates an inherent potential to change and dissolve natural relationships. If a hypothetical whitebark pine pop-

ulation came into contact with a better seed disperser, natural selection would favour the tree that evolved characteristics which would attract the new seed disperser even if the new traits caused the demise of its former mutualist, the Clark's nutcracker. A newly evolved bee might cause a flower to develop a morphology that would make it awkward for hummingbirds to work. Such changes can and do happen constantly as the world evolves.

If we lived longer and kept better records on the distributions of species, we would perceive the world as a more dynamic, fluctuating place. The notion that there is a balance of nature would never have occurred to beings who had seen aridity cycles, volcanic dust clouds and glacial episodes continually shifting and perturbing the natural world. In North America, the past 10,000 years alone — a trivial amount of time on the evolutionary scale — have seen forests march north and prairies spread east and then contract westward. During the vegetation changes, birds have continually come into contact with new species and changing combinations of species.

Ecologists conducting long-term studies are developing an understanding of the chaos in the natural world. Those who study natural bird communities have been steadily de-emphasizing the view that an ecological community is an integrated system with each component species fitting neatly into a balanced whole.

The Fortunes of Species

Perhaps the most ambitious of all bird-community studies is one conducted by Richard Holmes and Tom Sherry of Dartmouth College, in New Hampshire, and Franklin Sturgess of Shepherd College, in West Virginia. For 16 years, they studied a 25-acre area in the Hubbard Brook Experimental Forest, in New Hampshire. Each season, they took a census of the numbers and species of breeding birds, measured the abundance of caterpillars, a major food resource, and also kept track of changes in foliage density. They found significant variation in the community from year to year. As many as 28 bird species bred in some years and as few as 17 in others. The density of individuals shifted between a high of 214 and a low of 89. More important, the fortunes of species seemed to shift independently of each other. Outbreaks of caterpillars stimulated some species but not others; changes in foliage affected some species but not others; some species competed with other community members, but others did not seem to be affected by interspecific competition; some showed signs of being affected by winter weather but not others.

The complexity and lack of direct linkage between bird species led the researchers to conclude that what we perceive to be community structure is, in fact, a conglomerate of many largely independent processes. An ecological community is far from being a smoothly run machine with all the component species working in tight, well-oiled synchrony.

Such studies are few, but they are enough to indicate that there is much chaos and indeed an absence of rigid ecological bonding within natural communities. The findings make it difficult to justify retaining the idea of species diversity and pristine ecosystems in terms of necessary and harmonious interdependent relationships. Perhaps it is all to the good. Environmentalists have argued that preservationists who place utilitarian value on wildlife are mistaken. John A. Livingston points out in *The Fallacy of Wildlife Conservation* that economic development, rather than obscure plants and animals, is more readily favoured by utilitarian analyses and that we should not try to justify the existence of species by arguing the importance of their role in either the natural or the fiscal economy. Since ecological relationships are continually being formed and broken, a species could consequently be counted expendable by the criterion of ecological necessity.

Preservation of species and ecological relationships, then, must depend on a different set of values. I value the turkey vulture not because it is an essential scavenger that the forest must retain to stay

healthy. Rather, I am impressed by its ability to eat botulism with impunity and filth with evident gusto; I marvel that the ancestral precursor of the golden eagle has been shaped by natural selection into a bald-headed carrion hound; and I have laughed at a black vulture, an indignant clown in white spats, battling a dog for ownership of a sordid street corner in a banana-port town.

The naturalist's value system depends on personal contact with natural diversity, not on ecological necessity and utility. Our values are subjective and idiosyncratic. Hence my relationship with vultures is not like yours. The species that I treasure are not the same as the species you treasure. And that is why the preservation of species is a matter of self-preservation for every naturalist.

THE EMIGRANT FACTOR
A biologist's defence of a global perspective

North American birders praise the spectacle of our migratory birds on the move (left), yet many fail to realize that these migrations will become increasingly reduced as winter habitats are destroyed and bird populations subsequently decline.

My eyes downcast, I am fully occupied with my bit of the earth, watching the fork tines open the soil, exposing the potatoes like huge, pale eggs nested in the earth or stooping to waggle the carrots by their tops and to lift the bright orange tapers out of the dark and into the light. And then I hear the honking and calling in the north: above the trees, the first Canada geese are southbound. Their cries, the sound of their swishing wings and the sight of their long necks stretched in one collective direction express an urgency—as though they are chasing a fading sun that is receding from the Earth.

That is all repeated in the spring. Outside our house last April, I bent to pick up a Tennessee warbler, a bit of bright fluff with almost no mass to it—just enough to have broken its neck on one of our windows. The tiny warbler had spent 150 nights in a towering tropical forest, where rains come in torrents, where kinkajous and opossums prowl the treetops, where pit vipers wait. This warbler had crossed oceans, and now it was back—and dead. The dissonance made me realize that much of the marvel which is the first spring warbler is the sense of where it has been all winter long.

These things set me thinking about the shrinking tropical forest and the poisoned marshes of Chesapeake Bay. I have been wondering more and more about the autumn clouds and the arrows of southbound birds and the future of their destinations. The birds, the ecosystems and human societies are in trouble.

Even the sedentary northern naturalist must think of the larger ecological world beyond his or her own narrow sphere of activities. It is no accident that organizations seeking public donations for conservation programmes in the Tropics rely heavily on the example of migratory birds to make the issues seem relevant to North Americans. The bobolink that chortles in our waving hayfield makes the Argentinian pampas more real to me. The blackpoll warbler I see returning to its spruce forest in Quebec glows with Brazilian sunshine. The comings and goings of migratory birds link conti-

nents, and in the process, they expand our view of the world.

Broadening our perspective is becoming more and more necessary as the world grows smaller. In the current international economy, most of our actions have global ecological significance. The chain of cause and effect associated with our lives touches every bit of the globe and influences matters large and small: the pesticides we sell to other countries come home as residues in the fish we eat; the radioactivity of a French atomic test in Polynesia shows up in our caribou; a mighty leatherback sea turtle that hatched on a beach in Suriname chokes on a plastic bag it has mistaken for a jellyfish drifting south from the Canadian Arctic.

Not only are we capable of polluting a foreign land or organism, we can now consume its wildlife in a more direct manner. The incursion of multinational agribusiness into tropical environments, the clearcutting of trees and the devastation of the rain forest by squatters in search of fertile land have all had dire consequences. According to Oxford University's T.C. Whitmore, the globe's equatorial greenbelt is being destroyed relentlessly, at the rate of 75,000 acres per day. The cheap beef we feed our dogs and cats, more protein than

that eaten by the entire populace of India, is paid for with the destruction of tropical ecosystems. As we bite into a fast-food hamburger and wash it down with a carbonated sugar solution enlivened by kola nut extract and caffeine, another swath of tropical forest is being gutted to feed our demand for cheap tropical produce. As we eat, an ovenbird flies from one ecological wasteland to another, from pasture to plantation, seeking but not finding the trackless primeval tropical forest still imprinted in its genes as migratory maps.

Those things we do in innocence and ignorance are finally starting to come home in a tangible and unpleasant form: they are beginning to affect our migrant birds. The birds in our parks, forests and backyards, which we assume will show up as usual each spring, are in trouble. It is time for us to contemplate their winter.

An estimated five billion birds, at least 248 species in all, pour out of North America each autumn on their way to Central America and northern South America. They pack themselves into an area much smaller than the northern landmasses where they bred earlier, and so in winter, they exist at densities far greater than those of summer. Many of our northern songbirds

actually spend more time in tropical forests than in northern temperate habitats. For that reason alone, tropical ecology is part and parcel of the survival of our temperate songbirds. As a result, those ornithologists with tropical experience take a very different view of migration than do most northern naturalists, seeing it as an opportunity for tropical birds to increase their reproductive success in a summer location. From their point of view, these birds are migrating north for the temporary ease of a North American summer, rather than migrating south to avoid harsh, inhospitable winters.

Nevertheless, the objective scientific importance of the winter ecology of migrant birds has not been great enough to stimulate much research on the topic. Russell Greenberg of the Smithsonian Institution points out that it is only in this decade that ornithologists have actually shown territorial behaviour of migrants on their wintering grounds to be quite common. After reviewing everything published on the subject, Greenberg concludes that "the serious study of the ecology of migrant birds in tropical areas has barely begun."

Internationalists

It is relatively easy for an eastern North American ecologist employed by a government agency to obtain research funds to study ovenbirds breeding in temperate mixed deciduous forest. But if that person tries to complete the study by following the ovenbirds to the Neotropics, where they spend the majority of their days, the response will not be the same. Governments balk at the prospect of expending time and energy in a land beyond a border traced on a map. But birds are internationalists, and if we are to understand and preserve them, we, too, must be internationalists.

Ecologists and ornithologists cannot do credible research if they study only half the life history of an organism. And yet, despite the fact that there are few places left in the Tropics that are not within a day's flight of North America, most North American ornithologists have stayed at home while their subjects went south.

While birds such as the ovenbird (far left) breed in North American forests, they are dependent on the forest habitat in Central America, where they spend the winter. Much of that habitat has been destroyed to make room for agricultural crops such as coffee (above), which is a large component of the export market and currently takes up huge areas of Central and South America. The brown deforested hillsides in Costa Rica (right) were once covered with lush tropical forests that were home to a rich avifauna of resident birds as well as to migrant North American birds.

It was not until 1980 that the first collection of papers on the topic of migrant ecology in the Tropics was published. Browsing through that tome, one begins to realize that we have only begun to fathom the extent of the ecological complexity of the phenomenon of migrant birds that flutter around us every day of our temperate summers. I watch the first ruby-throated hummingbird working the columbines and know that a short while ago, the tiny bird was perhaps probing the flowers of a vine sprawled across the stelae and glyphs of a ruined Mayan civilization. But why Yucatán rather than Cuba or Jamaica? Who can assure me that as Central America's ecology is gradually destroyed, the ruby-throats will have the genetic flexibility to winter elsewhere?

Naturalists know enough to observe that even closely related species within the same genus show remarkably different patterns of movement. The grey vireo of the southwestern United States, for example, shifts just a little south into Mexico so that its winter and summer ranges are almost contiguous. But the Philadelphia vireos of boreal Canada take a large hop to a strip along the Pacific slope of Central America, the isthmus and Colombia. Jon Barlow of the Royal Ontario Museum, in Toronto, suggests that the migratory patterns are dictated by competition among the various vireos: each species journeys to and from habitats where competition with ecologically similar vireos is minimized. Perhaps that is the explanation. In any case, the pattern of vireo movement demonstrates a bewildering complexity.

Ornithologists are discovering unexpected richness in the tropical natural history of temperate birds. Who would have guessed that in winter, the eastern kingbird, a bird that I see all summer hawking insects along the lakeshore, enters into a special relationship with a tropical tree? Eugene Morton of the Smithsonian Institution points out that these kingbirds, along with red-eyed vireos and scarlet tanagers, begin their winter by flying deep into Amazonian Ecuador, Peru and Bolivia. They then follow the advancing dry season

north, apparently tracking the seasonal fruiting of the *Didymopanax morotonii*, a tree that is noted for relying on these birds to disperse its seeds. I will have to look with new eyes at the next crying kingbird that hovers over my trespassing canoe as it cruises by the overhanging cedars of Ontario's Lake Opinicon. It is a transmogrification of the Amazon forests.

The eastern wood peewee, another fly-

A few tropical birds, such as the sulphur-bellied flycatcher (far left), adjust well to forest clearing as long as a few trees remain. Others, like the red-lored parrot (above), which is completely dependent on tree fruit crops, are destroyed when a forest is cleared.

The prothonotary warbler (above), seen in Canadian and American forests, is thought of as a temperate bird. But it lives for only five months of the year in its northern range; the remaining time is spent in the lowland forests of Central and northern South America. Ill-suited for raising beef cattle, thousands of acres of cloud forest (far right) have nonetheless been partially cleared in an attempt to cash in on the North American demand for fast-food meat.

catcher that migrates to the same region, shows almost no interest in fruit. It continues to sally forth for insects from perches along the edges of forest openings. When John Fitzpatrick, a specialist in flycatchers, studied the peewee in Peru, he found that it had many of the same ecological habits as the vermilion flycatcher. But the vermilion flycatchers travelled to breed in Bolivia and Argentina when the peewees arrived, and they did not return to Amazonia until May, when the peewees had gone north. The timing of this sort of migration suggests a finely tuned competition.

It is an environmental disaster that so much intricate migrant ecology will be destroyed before we can begin to study it. Tropical forests cover only about 6 to 7 percent of the Earth, but they contain roughly two-thirds of all our bird species. Fifty acres of tropical forest are destroyed every minute of every hour of every day. As they disappear, many migrant bird populations must also decline.

Naturally, it is not just the birds that are in difficulty. Human poverty is increasing as habitats are degraded and the ecological productivity of the land diminishes. In the Tropics, we are witnessing the first terrifying demonstration that all species depend on the health of ecosystems. Ultimately, we all suffer when resources and species, humans included, are excessively exploited.

In proportion to their financial resources, knowledge and potential influence, North American scientists have done almost nothing about such ecological problems, leaving them instead to politicians and organizations consisting largely of untrained volunteers. Lester Short of the American Museum of Natural History has written, "It is ironical that we are blessed with a plethora of ornithologists having tremendous resources available to them in areas of the world where the fewest avian species occur, whereas there are few ornithologists with meagre resources in tropical regions where the most birds occur. . . . Many of us have opted for pure science, shying away from conservation, which is so often regarded as tainted by politics and somehow unclean!

I submit that ornithology now requires each of us to take an active role in the conservation of birds."

Limited Mental Geography

There is a curious disparity between what we know of the marvellous mechanisms of avian migration and what we know about the ecological systems in which the marvel takes place. It is amazing what scientists have discovered about bird migration and navigation. They have chartered planes during the day and the night, released birds and employed planetariums to show that birds can use the stars as compasses. They have built sophisticated instruments to discover and prove that birds can see ultraviolet light, which is invisible to us, and to show that birds can hear the deep ultrasound generated by winds pouring over the Rockies, sounds to which our ears are deaf. They have measured the effects of magnetic fields. They have borrowed the radar of the United States military to track migrants over great distances and to detect the role of wind pattern and cloud cover. They have analyzed the photoperiodic effect on the delicate hormonal balances within the blood and glands of birds that prompt the migratory urge. They have gathered astonishing information through dedication, work, intelligence and the use of sophisticated resources. And yet scientists as a group have made little use of their dedication, intelligence, energy and resources to preserve the ecosystems that sustain the very life they have studied so hard to be able to describe. Amateurs, naturalists and conservationists have done far more than academic biologists to protect bird populations.

We can only assume that a limited mental geography explains the chasm. Lester Short's remarks were written a mere four years ago. How late we have left it! Too many of the best-qualified individuals have stayed in the comfort of their ivory towers, clucking indignantly but impotently at the destruction. What is required is an activism that makes use of their skills and education. The most ordinary of industrial concerns, the most conservative fundamentalist reli-

gious groups, the watchdogs of consumer goods — all have lobby groups in the nation's capitals. But hordes of professional biologists sit back and complacently imagine that underfinanced conservation groups will somehow manage to publicize the crisis. If we are to do anything constructive about the fate of migrant birds, we have to understand that environmental devastation is driven by the politicians, planners and economists who remain stolidly urban and nationalistic, rather than ecological and global, in their outlook and who remain relatively uninformed and unaffected by ecologists.

Nor has the message of global interaction reached much of the general public. Not long ago, I was travelling on a plane from Toronto to Miami, where I planned to board another plane going south. Travelling next to me was a middle-aged American woman,

obviously well-to-do. We chatted, and she asked where I was headed. "Costa Rica," I replied. She looked puzzled. "Costa Rica . . . Costa Rica . . . Do we own that?"

Clearly, there are still North Americans who possess only the dimmest sense of international geography and of the potentially disastrous trends in global ecology that their lives determine. Yet the wealth and expertise that resides in the north can be used to build and rehabilitate the south only when the people in developed countries become more outward-looking. Ecologists in particular must use all their resources to make global ecological sustainability an integral part of our national- and foreign-policy agendas.

The restricted mental geography that our political nationalism promotes is what lends impetus to the decline of our own migrant

bird populations. They are the flagship of a larger fleet of troubles and may best be able to bring the message home in a tangible and appealing form. Perhaps the woman who confused Costa Rica and Puerto Rico would have more interest in them if she realized that their ecological degradation will impoverish the songbirds in her own backyard. The threatened loss of a few of our migratory wood warblers may motivate North Americans to save tropical forests that contain vast numbers of other resident species. From pure self-interest, temperate naturalists have plenty to be concerned about.

Princeton ecologist John Terborgh, an authority on Neotropical migrant birds, summarizes the deteriorating situation confronting our temperate songbirds: "About half of all land birds breeding in North

Tropical forest is not the only habitat that is disappearing. Wintering wetlands for migratory waterfowl (above) are being converted for agricultural use or being destroyed by pollution. The Cape May warbler (far right) is feeding on cocobola flowers along the shores of a Caribbean island. In the eastern United States, where summer breeding and feeding take place, this warbler is relatively well recognized, although little is known about how the bird passes the winter season.

America go to Mexico, the Bahamas, Cuba and Hispaniola. Migrants commonly make up 50 percent of bird numbers in these northern areas and lesser percentages as one goes south into southern Middle America. Since many migrants are concentrated in winter, the clearing of one hectare of forest in Mexico is probably equivalent to clearing five to eight hectares in the northeastern United States. . . . Continued tropical deforestation will result in major reductions in many species."

Nearly two-thirds of the birds that travel south from western North America pass through the interior of Mexico. That region has lost one-third of its forest in just the last two decades. The eastern birds that use Caribbean stopovers are even harder hit by deforestation. Such Caribbean islands as Hispaniola have been reduced to deserts —

denuded pastureland — rimmed by almost obscenely extravagant resorts along the coast. Haiti, for example, has only 3 percent of its forests left. Yet about two dozen species of our eastern woodland warblers rely on the area for overwintering.

Anthony Diamond of the Canadian Wildlife Service has recently made a detailed study of the expected habitat loss for many of the North American migrants. By the year 2000, a short dozen years from now, Philadelphia vireos will have lost 83 percent of their wintering habitat; ruby-throated hummingbirds, 59 percent; Baltimore orioles, 52 percent. The litany is long and depressing.

It is true that migrants often use edge habitats or early succession areas such as the forest that springs up along shifting riverbeds in Amazonia or near landslides in mountainous regions. But it is naïve to expect that birds which have evolved over thousands of years in virtually pristine tropical habitats will be able to cope effectively with the present rate of change. Terborgh argues that "the notion that second growth will provide a haven for migratory populations is, I think, largely fallacious. . . . Most migrants favour tree crowns or the cool dark recesses of the forest interior." In any case, second-growth forest is in short supply in Central America. In its place are huge areas of cattle pasture dominated by African grasses and pan-tropical weeds. "The total biomass of birds breeding in the North American continent will probably change little," suggests Ter-borgh. "What will change is the familiar ambience of our forests in springtime. It just won't sound the way it used to."

Even the temperate naturalist who lives where woodland is abundant and neigh-bours are a good way off will eventually be troubled by this phenomenon. The pall of tropical deforestation is already tainting our world, and the changes in our northern bird communities will intrude upon the most isolated northern naturalist. I used to thrill to the neon-blue flare of an indigo bunting as it passed from a hedgerow through a patch of sunlight. But now the buntings seem fraudulently abundant. I have learned that they are one of the species that thrives in the wastelands of Central America. Where once I took only delight in the sight and sound of one, I now notice that they seem to adorn every large sugar maple tree in May, and they are more like harbingers of decay than of ripening summer.

The tarnished source of the indigo bun-tings' fortunes makes the growing strength of their chorus sound increasingly like an anthem to tropical destruction and poverty. Their bright abundance is an eloquent expression of the corruption and misery wrought by politicians such as Somoza and Duvalier and those northern governments that have supported them. These tiny and beautiful birds are a sober admonition to us of the great and ugly consequences of our continuing indifference to the south.

BIRD WATCHING

Scholarship and fieldwork in the hands of amateurs

Uno and 4M are in Uno's southeast corner, down on the ground and in the weeds; Uno sings quite steadily from these positions—rapidly and not loudly. They pay no attention to me, although I am very near. Both are very much puffed out and even fly in this odd shape. 4M says nothing but follows Uno, going for him or after him every minute or so, but not fiercely; Uno merely flies a few feet. This keeps up for perhaps 10 minutes. Then 4M grows more belligerent and chases Uno around and about, and at last, they come to blows, falling to the ground and fighting furiously. They separate, and Uno sings in the Norway maple, while 4M goes to his box elder. Each sings and sings.

Fragments from a landmark study on male song sparrows, these observations revolutionized the way birds were studied. The research itself was significant science. But the life of the author, amateur bird watcher Margaret Nice, was of even greater importance to the future of natural science in general and bird watching in particular.

Born Margaret Morse in 1883 in Amherst, Massachusetts, Nice's roots were in academia, her father being a history professor at the college in Amherst. At age 18, she enrolled in Mount Holyoke College and spent five years earning a bachelor's degree in science. Unlike most women of the time, she persisted with her research even after marrying a professor and becoming the mother of five daughters.

The demands of five children and marriage to another academic might easily have ended Nice's involvement with science. But she earned a master's degree in child psychology from Clark University in 1915 and published 18 papers on child psychology. At the same time, she and her husband began a survey of the birds of Oklahoma that was published in 1924.

Eventually, Nice focused her research solely on birds. In her autobiography, appropriately titled *Research Is a Passion With Me*, Nice recalls the walk she took one August day that led her away from the life of the conventional housewife and away

An amateur birder scans the shoreline of Ontario's Point Pelee National Park, a famous stopover for migrating songbirds (left). Birding has become the most popular and well-organized branch of natural history and is a field where amateurs can make substantial scientific contributions.

145

This group of avid birders (above), using powerful scopes and binoculars to search for shorebirds, is involved in a quest that is often social and intensely competitive. In addition to their urge to see new species, birding organizations gather data on changing geographic distributions, breeding densities, patterns of migration and other information on avian ecology. Millions of people describe themselves as "birders" and display a fanatic devotion to their hobby (left). Harnessing their enthusiasm in order to collect scientifically useful information and to increase our understanding of birds is one of the purposes of ornithological associations.

from child psychology: "Under the great elms and cottonwoods on the riverbank, I watched the turbulent Canadian River and dreamed. The glory of nature possessed me. I saw that for many years, I had lost my way. I had been led astray on false trails and had been trying to do things contrary to my nature. I resolved to return to my childhood vision of studying nature and trying to protect the wild things of the earth."

When the Nices moved to Columbus, Ohio, Margaret was reborn as a naturalist. Her resolve took a form that most people must have considered eccentric. She devoted eight years of her life to a study of the song sparrows nesting in the tangled fields and brush around her house. She began gradually, setting a small shelf trap near her house and colour-banding a few birds so that she could recognize them as individuals. Nice's interest in the details of their lives began to grow. She found out that "the men at the State Museum, fine field naturalists and well acquainted with the local birds, could not answer my questions." So she struck out on her own, with unorthodox methods.

Working a few hours every day, she banded the sparrows and laboriously mapped their territories. She noted when they returned, when they sang, how females chose territories, which males won fights, who mated with whom, how many offspring they fledged, where the banded young dispersed, the effect of cowbird brood parasitism and how weather affected these events. And she continued on, year after year, building up a lifetime profile of individuals and a population. Nice eventually banded and followed the fortunes of 136 individuals, learning to recognize many by the distinctive elements of their songs. Some were prodigies like 4M, who returned for a total of nine years; others were failures.

At a time when territoriality was still an unproven concept, Nice was the first to document the tremendous long-term fidelity of males to breeding territories. She showed that females also defended territories against other females but that from year to year, or even within a summer, they often changed mates and territories. The result of her detailed observations was a tour de force with a depth and vision unmatched in the ornithology of the time.

Nice did not meet with immediate acclaim from professional science. Unable to find a U.S. publisher for her massive study, she finally received an offer from a German ornithological journal. After the appearance of her work in German, the Linnaean Society in New York agreed to publish it in English under the title *Studies in the Life History of the Song Sparrow*.

Once it was published, her account had a great impact. The second volume appeared in 1943, the same year Joseph Hickey (who characterized bird watching as "a mild paralysis of the nervous system, which can only be cured by rising at dawn and sitting in a bog") published his popular book *A Guide to Bird Watching*. Hickey said of Nice's work, " No other life-history study combines such rich scholarship with such keen fieldwork" and touted it as "an indispensable reference work for bird watchers and ornithologists."

Other ornithologists went even further in their praise. Erwin Stresemann, the Berlin ornithologist who in 1951 reviewed the entire history of ornithology, considered Nice's work to be "pioneering" because "for the first time, it was possible to follow the fate of individual birds from birth to death, determine exactly their fertility rate, examine their relation to other members of the same population and obtain much information about which there had previously been only the vaguest notions."

On the Cutting Edge

Research is a social activity, and even the most innovative practitioners depend to some extent on role models. In her writing, Nice often credits another amateur, H. Eliot Howard, as a source of ideas. Although Aristotle and various observers after him had noted territorial defence of an area by birds, it was Howard who made the concept well known among ornithologists.

Howard went to work each day as director of a steel-manufacturing plant in England, but he had an avid interest in the birds in his own backyard. He mapped lapwing territories along the Severn River and observed reed buntings in the marshes near his house. Howard did not gather detailed data, but his book on territoriality is based on a balanced weighing of theory against observation. It was a sophisticated approach. In developing the concept of territoriality, he was concerned with the issues of semantics, anthropomorphism and observer bias. The opening quotation in his book *Territory in Bird Life* cautioned that "human language is especially constructed to describe the mental states of human beings, and this means that it is especially constructed to mislead us when we attempt to describe the working of minds that differ from the human." The result of his thought and observation was a carefully argued exposition that firmly established the importance of territoriality.

The strides Nice and Howard made can perhaps be best judged by a comparison with a popular ornithological book still in circulation at the time, *Wake Robin* by John Burroughs. In his last chapter, Burroughs gives a famous recipe for bird study: "First, find your bird; observe its ways, its song, its calls, its flight, its haunts; then shoot it (not ogle it with a glass); and compare with Audubon. In this way, the feathered kingdom may soon be conquered."

What distinguished Nice and Howard was their goal: to unravel the process and develop hypotheses to explain not only what birds are doing but why they behave as they do. They thought about birds as living, dynamic entities. It is in this sense that these two amateurs bridged the gap between the 19th-century naturalist and 20th-century science. Nice and Howard were naturalists whose work in natural history was on the cutting edge of scientific discovery.

Nice and Howard were much closer to an era in which a great deal of natural science was still conducted by "amateurs" — people whose income was derived from sources other than the science in which they worked. J.P. Burkitt, who in the 1930s used techniques similar to Nice's, showed

The weight of this thick-billed murre chick provides biologist Erick Greene (above) with information on food availability and the growth rate of this population of Arctic seabirds. Most ecological studies of populations depend on thousands of time-consuming measurements, which means that volunteers can often be of assistance. Ecologist Bruce Lyon has suspended himself over a precipitous rock face as he studies nesting thick-billed murres (far right), demonstrating the high degree of commitment required by some kinds of field study.

that robin territories are based on a geometry of hedges, the length of the border hedge being more important than the area. A county surveyor in Ireland, he nonetheless published scientific papers on his observations. Writing in 1943 about the usefulness of amateur bird-banders, Joseph Hickey observed: "Most of these are laymen. . . . Some of the most famous banders have been women: Mrs. Margaret M. Nice in Ohio, Mrs. Mabel Gillespie in Pennsylvania, Mrs. F.C. Laskey in Tennessee, Mrs. Kenneth B. Wetherbee in New England, Mrs. Harold Michener in California, Mrs. Marie V. Beals in New York and Mrs. F.M. Baumgartner now of Oklahoma. Their combined scientific papers would do credit to the staff of any museum or experimental station." Arthur Cleveland Bent, whose compilation of North American bird-life histories is still the most complete collection in existence, was also an amateur, earning his living by manufacturing textiles in New England.

Professional Monopoly

Research was the avocation of this group of people, and they were accepted in this role as a valued part of science. But serious science was becoming more and more the exclusive province of employees of universities and museums; in the 20th century, the involvement of amateurs in science has decreased proportionately. It is difficult to identify a group of amateurs that makes a contribution comparable to that of a research institution. This is understandable in expensive branches of biology such as cellular physiology and biochemical genetics, but the modus operandi of behavioural ecology differs little from that developed by Nice 50 years ago.

What enlarged the gap between natural historians and academic biologists? Academics seem to encourage the separation. Forty years ago, conservationist Aldo Leopold observed that "ornithology, mammalogy and botany as now known to most amateurs are but kindergarten games compared with what is possible for (and open to) amateurs in these fields. One

reason for this is that the whole structure of biological education (including education in wildlife) is aimed at perpetuating the professional monopoly on research."

In defining their own niche, some academics seek to differentiate their scientific endeavours from those of natural history. Robert Peters, an ecologist at McGill University, in Montreal, argues that natural history and ecology are fundamentally different. According to Peters, "The goal of biology, ecology or any science is prediction. . . . To a scientist, understanding implies prediction, whereas the understanding of a naturalist is an empathy with nature."

We must reject such a false dichotomy. For modern naturalists, understanding, prediction and empathy coexist. Understanding the evolutionary and ecological explanations of natural phenomena does not diminish but, rather, deepens our empathy and increases our perception. Ecologists who cannot empathize with their subjects are destined to produce uninspired science. Indeed, physiological ecologist George Bartholomew of the University of California has reasoned that biologists who lack a general grounding in natural history often end up doing unproductive research because they are unaware of the real-world adaptive context and larger significance of the smaller phenomena they are analyzing.

In any case, a science of ecology that does not address the human interaction with nature is grossly deficient as an explanatory tool. Evolutionary biologist Michael Ghislen comments as a scientist: "We tend to treat science as strictly impersonal, the product of objective methodology dealing with the observed facts. Yet scientists are like everybody else and cannot utterly divorce their values from their professions. . . . This habit of depersonalizing science gives a false impression of how scientific research is done." The greatest evolutionary biologists and ecologists, such as Charles Darwin, Ernst Mayr, Robert MacArthur and G.E. Hutchinson, were all well versed in natural history in its broadest sense. Their ideas did not arise in a vacuum, nor did

they develop according to mathematical formulas. Their ideas came from many sources – readings, thoughts and conversations – and often as a result of witnessing natural events. The response of these men to nature was as much a part of the fabric and interest of science as the predictive laws they discovered.

Misguided Elitist Notion

While certain academics may imagine that a predictive generalization is their ultimate contribution to ecology, other biologists see a growing need to document and account for the special cases that make up our world. The latter preoccupation remains the province of natural historians. Generalization *is* a major goal of science. But as theoretical ecologist Richard Levins has observed, "General models are necessary but not sufficient for understanding nature. For understanding is not achieved by generality alone, but by a relation between the general and the particular."

In the search for the generalities of science, we should not forget a fundamental feature of the natural world we study: it is composed of millions of species, each of which has shared not only general properties but unique ones as well. Every species has its own history, its own habits, its own distinct genes. In Bartholomew's words, "It is time we biologists accept diversity and variability for what they are, two of the essential features of the biological world. . . . Because of its focus on organisms, natural history is in a unique position to supply questions and integrating links among disciplines."

Natural history is an evolving science that requires the broadest possible amateur participation, because it includes field observation, ecological experiments, the data of physiological ecology – in fact, any information or approach which helps explain the natural world. I recall the image of a flock of evening grosbeaks descending on the red clouds of swamp holly. The same forest carries the displays of bittersweet, poison ivy and clusters of ash seeds waiting to escape on the wind. What will we harvest

from this spectacle beyond the blur of pigments? To understand and appreciate the interaction between these birds and plants, we need naturalists willing to watch the fruit selection of autumn flocks of birds. We require a systematic botanist who will explain the evolutionary relationships among the plants that have become bird-dispersed. We need an ecologist to assess the reproductive benefits the plants gain from fruit dispersal. We must ask a biochemist to analyze the nutrient content of the fruit and have a physiologist tell us the diet a migrating bird needs in terms of fats, sugars and vitamins.

There is a real opportunity for reciprocity between professional scientist and amateur natural historian. Ecology and the study of behaviour are usually labour-intensive disciplines. For those who do not wish to strike out on their own, there are plenty of researchers who need assistance. And academics can offer valuable guidance about areas and methods of research.

Let us dispose of any misguided elitist notion that science is just for professional academics. It is too important for that. Hickey suggested that bird study in the first part of the 20th century saw two revolutions: the use of binoculars, rather than shotguns, for identification; and the spread of bird-banding. We need a third revolution: a popular movement in behavioural ecology that will put the vast public interest in nature to use. Evolutionary biology and ecology should be taught as though they are as fundamental to our education as the laws of gravity and geometry. We need to increase the rate at which knowledge is gathered and diffused to people. Species and habitats are disappearing faster than academics can study them, and that can be attributed largely to an astonishing ignorance of ecology in the majority of the population and to our estrangement from science.

A huge scientific resource is virtually untapped because of the separation between the amateur and the professional scientist. There are tens of millions of enthusiastic, intelligent bird watchers, but the energy that makes them rise at 5 a.m.,

trudge through swamps and travel thousands of miles a year is largely untapped by science. Instead, that energy is translated into lists of species seen, records of rare birds, Christmas counts and breeding-bird surveys through organized birding clubs. That work has some use as an indicator of environmental change, but too often, the questions amateurs address and the methods they use are dated or ill-defined primarily because of the lack of contact with scientists. The contribution of energetic birding groups would be of much greater value if there were a more meaningful interaction between the academic and the amateur.

Still, there is always room for the independent approach. It is not true that one needs a doctorate, a job in academia or a large research grant to participate in

Pristine surroundings, like the wetland area in which this birder makes her observations (above), provide one of the greatest attractions of bird study. Coloured plastic leg bands (right) enable bird banders to mark and identify hundreds of thousands of birds individually each year. Recovery and resightings provide ecologists with the fundamental information on population composition, survival and dispersal rates needed to detect changes in bird populations and in the environment.

The bander holding this Christmas Island warbler (above) will take valuable data on the bird's weight and body size before banding and releasing the bird. The spectacular, often abundant and easy-to-observe bald eagle (right) is typical of most birds in that many aspects of its behaviour and ecology remain a fertile terra incognita awaiting exploration by both amateur and professional ornithologists.

science. Anyone who can read and has some enthusiasm is eligible. Nor is behavioural ecology expensive: the vast majority of it requires only the simplest of equipment, which bird watchers usually already possess—a watch, a notebook, binoculars and little else.

The backyard or the nearest woodlot will do for a study site. Just as Thoreau found he could travel far in Concord, Howard and Nice made their contributions by working alongside their dwellings. Every researcher will find that the most commonplace organisms are virtually terra incognita. Not long ago, I read an interesting paper about robins in a leading scientific journal. One of its findings was that robin pairs divide their territories in half along the east-west axis while foraging for food. The male always searches in one half, the female in the other,

an arrangement that maximizes food extraction while minimizing competition between the paired male and female. This discovery, one that implies a coordinated, sophisticated division of territory and sense of territorial geography, was made with minimal equipment and expense by an individual observing four pairs of robins on a college campus in Kansas.

Let me give as another example the work of Lawrence Kilham. By profession, Kilham works in the microbiology department of Dartmouth Medical School, but he has made a large contribution to ornithology. Over the past three decades, he has produced a steady stream of papers about the behaviour of pileated, hairy and downy woodpeckers and yellow-bellied sapsuckers. One might expect that birds as common as these would be well studied; yet Kilham

is documenting new aspects of their behavioural ecology. He has discovered how woodpeckers use calling and drumming to communicate. He has looked at the territorial behaviour of pairs of male and female woodpeckers and found that downies pair-bond only during breeding season, while pileateds remain together and territorial year-round, a difference that Kilham argues is related to the different types of food these species require. Pileateds feed on stable food supplies like carpenter-ant colonies and beetle larvae that are found deep in tree trunks. They can exploit the sources year-round in their territories. Downies, by contrast, feed on small, superficially located and patchy concentrations of insects. In winter, when food is generally scarce, downies abandon their territories and range about, cleaning up rich areas of food and then moving on to others. Kilham has helped us realize the ecological and behavioural diversity exhibited by our common woodpeckers. There is hardly a walk I have taken in an eastern deciduous forest that has not been enriched for me by Kilham's work on woodpeckers.

In addition to bolstering our knowledge about common birds, naturalists can afford to work on the less fashionable and logistically difficult but still valuable aspects of natural history. Because natural history is a pleasure and not a career strategy for them, amateurs can do research that is incompatible with the demands of acquiring tenure and getting grants. Academia does not reward ecologists who simply walk out in their woodlots and make careful observations. Today's academic focus is on experimental hypothesis testing and a high rate of publication. This emphasis means that plain observation, the a priori documentation of nature which generates meaningful theories and which must precede hypothesis testing, receives little attention. Amateurs can take their time and do long-term research unconstrained by the pressure to publish or perish. That is what an understanding of avian diversity demands. There are rare birds about which it takes a long time to amass publishable data; there are birds that are active during the academic teaching season; and there are birds that are hard to observe because of their unusual habits. These are the species that amateurs can afford to study.

Naturally, it is not reasonable to expect that every naturalist will want to do research, but it is impossible to deny the existence of a strong, untapped interest. The organizations that cater to people wishing to pay to become assistants on field projects are thriving and expanding. I have often made use of their services and have been impressed by how many people are attracted to research. At the same time, I am depressed by the fact that so many talented, educated people have passed their entire lives without ever having believed they were capable of doing their own invaluable work.

Reflect on the large number of small contributions that more amateur participation in science could generate. These modest contributions are the foundation of Western science and are especially important in a world that may have as many as 30 million distinct animal and plant species. Anyone who doubts the role that amateur naturalists can play in science should recall that the most important work on this world of special cases is still Darwin's *The Origin of Species*, a book that emerged from thousands of synthesized tidbits of natural history studied and reported, in large part, by other amateur naturalists. The observations of these naturalists helped build the most profound document of all time: an explanation of what we are and how we came to be, a general theory that finally made sense of the living universe. Long may their work continue.

SOURCES

The range of literature on ornithology, both scientific and popular, is vast. I will suggest only a few works to encourage the enthusiast and some outstanding and lesser known works that I believe should have wider circulation.

By and large, ornithology textbooks do not mention many of the new ideas in behavioural ecology. Good introductions to behavioural ecology can be found in:

Animal Behavior, An Evolutionary Approach, John Alcock. Sunderland: Sinauer Associates, 1979.

An Introduction to Behavioral Ecology, J.R. Krebs and N.B. Davies. Oxford: Blackwell Scientific Publications, 1981.

Sociobiology: The New Synthesis, E.O. Wilson. Cambridge, Massachusetts: Harvard University Press, 1975.

General ornithology texts include:

Fundamentals of Ornithology, J. van Tyne and A.J. Berger. New York: Wiley, 1976.

An Introduction to Ornithology, G. Wallace and H.D. Mahan. New York: The Macmillan Company, 1975.

The Life of Birds, J.C. Welty. Philadelphia: W.B. Saunders Company Ltd., 1975.

A more enjoyable read containing much of the basic information but presented with less rigorous science and enlivened with personal observation and philosophic reflection is *The Adventure of Birds* by Charlton Ogburn (New York: Morrow, 1980).

More detailed treatment of general topics in bird ecology and behaviour can also be found in books such as:

Avian Ecology and Behaviour, C.M. Perrins. Glascow: Blackie, 1983.

The Growth and Development of Birds, R.J. O'Connor. New York: Wiley, 1984.

Parent Birds and Their Young, A.F. Skutch. Austin: University of Texas Press, 1976.

Perspectives in Ornithology, A.H. Brush and G.A. Clark Jr. New York: Cambridge University Press, 1983.

A Guide to the Behavior of Common Birds, D.W. Stokes. Boston: Little Brown, 1979.

Bird Behavior, R. Burton. London: Granada, 1985.

A.C. Bent's *Life Histories of North Ameri-*

The downward-bent bills of these adult flamingos and their young (left) are their most remarkable feature, allowing them to scoop up organic matter on the bottom of the pond where they are feeding and to sift through it to find the food they want.

can Birds, 23 volumes of which were published by New York's Peter Smith and Dover between 1919 and 1968, are still essential.

More modern information on avian biology can be found in *Avian Biology, Current Ornithology, Annual Review of Ecology and Systematics.*

Several excellent massive encyclopaedic texts on birds have recently been published. Most notable are:
The Encyclopedia of Birds, edited by C.M. Perrins and A.L.A. Middleton. New York: Facts on File, 1985.
A Dictionary of Birds, edited by B. Campbell and E. Lack. Vermillion, South Dakota: Buteo Books, 1985.

Many quarterly journals specialize in birds, and these include *The Auk, Ibis* and *Living Bird Quarterly.* Some of the best work on birds is now published in more general journals such as *Animal Behavior, Ecology* and *Behavioral Ecology.*

There are many books of a more general sort that contain reflections on the nature and meaning of bird life. These include:
A Sand County Almanac, Aldo Leopold. New York: Oxford University Press, 1949.
Sonoran Desert Spring, John Alcock. Chicago: University of Chicago Press, 1985.
Idle Days in Patagonia, W.H. Hudson. London: Dent, 1893.
Keith County Journal, John Janovy. New York: St. Martin's, 1978.
Natural Acts, A Sidelong View of Science and Nature, David Quammen. New York: Dell, 1985.

Finally, I have indicated one or two key references for most chapters:

Nests

Alexander Skutch's *Parent Birds and Their Young*, published in 1976 by the University of Texas Press, has many original observations on birds' nests. For a recent review of nest-building behaviour, see N. and E. Collias' *Nest Building & Bird Behavior*, published by Princeton University Press in 1984.

Beauty

Darwin's treatise *The Descent of Man and Selection in Relation to Sex* ranks as one of the great books of all time and should be read by every naturalist. Mary Jane West-Eberhard's paper in *The Quarterly Review of Biology*, Volume 58, pages 155-183, is a recent treatment of the topic of sexual and social selection. There are two excellent papers on bowerbirds: one by Jared Diamond in the journal *Ethology*, 74, pages 177-204; and the other by Gerald Borgia in the journal *Behavioral Ecology and Sociobiology*, 18, pages 91-100. E.O. Wilson's collection of essays entitled *Biophilia*, published by Harvard University Press, 1986, contains an excellent discussion on the relationship between art and science.

Song

How Animals Communicate, by Thomas A. Sebeok (Indiana University Press, 1975), provides a panoramic view of bird communication through song.

Mating

See *Ecological Aspects of Social Evolution: Birds and Mammals*, edited by D. Rubenstein and R. Wrangham (Princeton University Press, 1986), and *Mate Choice*, edited by Patrick Bateson (Cambridge University Press, 1983).

Colonies

For a recent review, see the article on avian coloniality by J.F. Whittenberger and G.L. Hunt in *Avian Biology*, Volume VIII, pages 1-78, 1985.

Propaganda

Behavioral Ecology: An Evolutionary Approach, edited by J. Krebs and N. Davies (Sinauer Associates, 1984), contains a useful chapter that discusses communication as manipulation.

Images

One Man's Owl by Bernd Heinrich (Princeton University Press, 1987) takes an intelligent look at the interactions of owls with other birds. His work on chickadees is reported in his autobiographical *In a Patch of Fireweed* (Harvard University Press, 1984). *Mimicry in Plants and Animals* by Wolfgang Wickler (McGraw-Hill, 1968) is a well-illustrated survey of mimicry.

Intelligence

Animal Intelligence: Insights into the Animal Mind, edited by R.J. Hoage and Larry Goldman (Smithsonian, 1986), is a recent survey of animal intelligence and learning. *The Growth and Development of Birds* by Raymond J. O'Connor (Wiley, 1984) summarizes the literature on learning in birds.

Ignoble Nature

The Selfish Gene by Richard Dawkins (Oxford University Press, 1976) is the single best exposition on "gene thinking." S. Rhower's article on infanticide in *Current Ornithology*, Volume 3, is a recent and novel review of the topic.

Relationships

Ecological Communities — Conceptual Issues and the Evidence, edited by D.R. Strong Jr., D. Simberloff, L. Abele and A. Thistle (Princeton University Press, 1984), is a collection of papers that shows the strength of the differences in the way ecologists conceive of ecological community structure. *Coevolution*, a collection of papers edited by Douglas Futuyma and Montgomery Satkin (Sinauer Associates, 1983), is the most complete work on the topic of coevolution. See also the paper by R. Holmes and T. Sherry in *Ecological Monographs*, 56, pages 201-220, for a recent review of avian community ecology. *The Fallacy of Wildlife Conservation* by John Livingston (McClelland and Stewart, 1981) is a passionate exposition of the argument against a utilitarian conservationist strategy.

The Emigrant Factor

Migrant Birds in the Neotropics: Ecology, Behavior, Distribution and Conservation, edited by Alan Keast and Eugene Morton, Smithsonian Institution, 1980.

Bird Watching

George Bartholomew's article "The Role of Natural History in Contemporary Biology" appeared in *Bioscience* magazine in May 1986.

INDEX

Acanthis flammea. See Redpoll
Accipiter striatus. See Hawk, sharp-shinned
Aeronautes saxatalis. See Swift,
   white-throated
Agelaius phoeniceus. See Blackbird,
   red-winged
Alarm calling, 88-91
Albatross, 57, 58
   black-browed (*Diomedea melanophris*),
     illus., 40, 57
   Laysan (*Diomedea immutabilis*),
     illus., 110
Alcock, John, 130
Amateur work in natural history, 145-153
Amazona autumnalis. See Parrot,
   red-lored
Amblyornis inoratus. See Bowerbird,
   Vogelkop
Ameiva lizard, 107
Ampelion stresemanni. See Cotinga,
   white-cheeked
Anas platyrhynchos. See Mallard duck
Anastomus oscitans. See Stork, Asian
   open-bill
Anhinga (*Anhinga anhinga*), illus., 26
Ani, groove-billed (*Crotophaga sulcirostris*),
   115
Anser caerulescens. See Goose, snow
Antbird, 53
Antshrike, bluish-slate (*Thamnomanes
   schistogynus*), 90-91
Aphelocoma coerulescens. See Jay, scrub
Aptenodytes patagonicus. See Penguin, king
Apus apus. See Swift, common
Aquila chrysaetos. See Eagle, golden
Ara macao. See Macaw, scarlet
Archilochus colubris. See Hummingbird,

ruby-throated
Ardea herodias. See Heron, great blue
Asio flammeus. See Owl, short-eared
Aulacorhynchus prasinus. See Toucanet,
   emerald
Baldridge, R.S., 22
Balearica. See Crane, crowned
Barlow, Jon, 139
Bartholomew, George, 148, 150
Bates, Henry, 101
Bates, Marston, 122
Beauty, 29-41
   in bird song, 43-44, 49, 53
Bellbird, 130
   three-wattled (*Procnias tricarunculata*),
     92
Bennett, Peter, 107
Bent, Arthur Cleveland, 148
Bewick, Thomas, 114
Bird of paradise, 45, 70
Bird watchers, 145-153
Black, Hal, 107
Blackbird, 111; illus., 81
   red-winged (*Agelaius phoeniceus*), 21,
     49, 51, 65, 66, 70, 71, 80, 92, 100,
     101; illus., 20-21, 32-33, 50, 93
   yellow-headed (*Xanthocephalus
     xanthocephalus*), illus., 44-45
Bluebird (*Sialia*), 26, 65, 113-114
Bobolink (*Dolichonyx oryzivorus*), 58,
   65, 135
Bonasa umbellus. See Grouse, ruffed
Borgia, Gerald, 34-36, 45-47
Bowerbird, 34-36, 45. See also Calf bird,
   spotted
   Lauterbach's (*Chlamydera lauterbachi*),
     illus., 34

satin (*Ptilonorhynchus violaceus*), 34-36
   Vogelkop (*Amblyornis inoratus*), 34
Bowers, purpose of, 34-36
Branta canadensis. See Goose, Canada
Breland, Marian, 109, 111
Brower, Jane and Lincoln, 101-102
Brown, Charles, 82-83
Bubo virginianus. See Owl, great horned
Bubulcus ibis. See Egret, cattle
Budgerigar (*Melopsittacus undulatus*), 111
Bulbul, 45
Bunting, 49
   indigo (*Passerina cyanea*), 64, 65,
     92, 143
   painted (*Passerina ciris*), 31
   snow (*Plectrophenax nivalis*), 116
   yellow, 99
Buphagus. See Oxpecker
Burkitt, J.P., 147-148
Buteo platypterus. See Hawk, broad-winged
Butorides spp. See Heron
Cacique, yellow-rumped (*Cacicus cela*),
   66-68
Caldwell, Gloria, 100
Calf bird, spotted (*Perissocephalus tricolor*),
   38
Campylopterus hemileucurus. See
   Hummingbird, violet sabre-wing
Canary (*Serinus canaria*), 51
Caracara, black (*Daptrius ater*), 68
Cardinal (*Cardinalis cardinalis*), 52
Carduelis spp. See Goldfinch; Siskin, pine
Carpodacus purpureus. See Finch, purple
Catbird, 21
Cathartes aura. See Vulture, turkey
Catharus spp. See Thrush
Centrocercus urophasianus. See Grouse,

sage
Cephalopterus glabricollis. See Umbrella
   bird, bare-necked
Chaetura pelagica. See Swift, chimney
Chapman, Frank, 113
Charadrius vociferus. See Killdeer
Chickadee (*Parus*), 26, 38, 105, 109
   black-capped (*Parus atricapillus*), 65,
     89-90, 103; illus., 37
Chicken, 105, 106, 109
   prairie (*Tympanuchus cupido*), illus., 69,
     112
Chlamydera lauterbachi. See Bowerbird,
   Lauterbach's
Chlorophonia (*Chlorophonia*), 128
Circus cyaneus. See Harrier, northern
Cistothorus spp. See Wren
Clangula hyemalis. See Old-squaw duck
Clark, Karen, 21
Clark, Larry, 22
Clay, Teresa, 77
Cockatoo, 105
Cock-of-the-rock, Guianan (*Rupicola
   rupicola*), 69
Colinvaux, Paul, 125-127
Colonies, 73-85
Communication, 87-94
Competition among birds, 113-119,
   125-128
Condor, Andean (*Vultur gryphus*), 58
Contopus virens. See Peewee, eastern wood
Cooke, Fred, 64
Coragyps atratus. See Vulture, black
Corvus spp. See Crow; Raven
Cotinga, 45
   white-cheeked (*Ampelion stresemanni*),
     128

Cotingids, 69, 70
Courtship and mating, 55-71
Cowbird, 13, 21, 32
Crane, crowned (*Balearica*), illus., 35
    Manchurian (*Grus japonensis*), illus., 46
Crocker, D.R., 119
Crossbill (*Loxia*), 131; illus., 132
Crotophaga sulcirostris. See Ani,
    groove-billed
Crow (*Corvus*), 59, 80, 105, 108
Curio, Eberhard, 111
Cyanocitta cristata. See Jay, blue
Cypseloides niger. See Swift, black
Cypsiurus parvus. See Swift, palm
Dacnis, scarlet-thighed (*Dacnis venusta*),
    118
Daptrius ater. See Caracara, black
Darwin, Charles, 16, 29-30, 32-33, 49,
    53, 74, 119, 148, 153
Dawkins, Richard, 114
Deception in bird communication, 90-92
Dendrogapus canadensis. See
    Grouse, spruce
Dendroica spp. See Warbler
Diamond, Anthony, 142
Diamond, Jared, 34
Dicaeum hirundinaceum. See
    Mistletoe bird
Diomedea spp. See Albatross
Dolichonyx oryzivorus. See Bobolink
Dove, white-winged (*Zenaida asiatica*),
    illus., 27
Dromaius novaehollandiae. See Emu
Dryocopus pileatus. See Woodpecker,
    pileated
Duck, mallard (*Anas platyrhynchos*),
    illus., 71
    old-squaw (*Clangula hyemalis*), 21
Eagle, bald (*Haliaeetus leucocephalus*), 22;
    illus., 45, 84, 86, 153
    golden (*Aquila chrysaetos*), 116, 133
    harpy (*Harpia harpyia*), 58
Ecological relationships, 121-133
Ecological systems, nature of, 121-133
Egret, illus., 6, 129
    cattle (*Bubulcus ibis*), illus., 123
    great (*Egretta alba*), 100; illus., 70
    snowy (*Egretta thula*), 100
Egretta spp. See Egret
Eibl-Eibesfeldt, 114
Emu (*Dromaius novaehollandiae*), 105,
    106; illus., 107
Eumomota superciliosa. See Motmot,
    turquoise-browed
Eurypyga helias. See Sunbittern
Evans, Roger, 82
Eye images, 97-99
Falco spp. See Gyrfalcon, snow-white;
    Kestrel
Feeding behaviour and intelligence,
    107-111
Feinsinger, Peter, 125
Finch, 128
    purple (*Carpodacus purpureus*), 131
Fisher, Ronald, 36
Fitzpatrick, John, 140
Flamingo, American (Caribbean)
    (*Phoenicopterus ruber*), illus., 78-79
Florida caerulea. See Heron, little blue
Flycatcher, 49
    ash-throated (*Myiarchus cinerascens*),
    illus., 96
    great crested (*Myiarchus crinitus*), 25

sulphur-bellied (*Myiodynastes luteiventris*),
    illus., 138
    tropical, 21
    vermilion (*Pyrocephalus rubinus*), 140
Fogden, Michael, 92
Foraging techniques in colonies, 80-85
Fratercula arctica. See Puffin, Atlantic
Freeman, Scott, 92
Frigate bird (*Fregata*), 57-58
Gallinula. See Moorhen
Gallus gallus. See Jungle fowl, red
Gannet (*Sula bassana*), 65; illus., 62-63,
    64, 75
Gaston, Tony, 80-82
Gavia. See Loon
Gehlback, F.R., 22
Ghislen, Michael, 148
Gillard, Thomas, 34
Goldfinch (*Carduelis*), 31-32; illus., 31,
    126
Goose, 105, 111
    Canada (*Branta canadensis*), 135;
    illus., 116-117, 117
    snow (*Anser caerulescens*), 64; illus.,
    12-13
Goshawk, 65; illus., 12
Gowaty, Patricia, 113
Grackle, 101
    boat-tailed (*Quiscalus major*), 31
Grebe, red-necked (*Podiceps grisegena*),
    illus., 18, 65
Greenberg, Russell, 108, 136
Greene, Erick, 84-85, 148
Grinnel, Joseph, 131
Grosbeak, 131
    evening (*Hesperiphona vespertina*), 150
Grouse, 91
    ruffed (*Bonasa umbellus*), 9, 55-56, 57;
    illus., 54
    sage (*Centrocercus urophasianus*), 56, 69;
    illus., 8, 56
    sharp-tailed (*Tympanuchus phasianellus*),
    56
    spruce (*Dendrogapus canadensis*), 55-56
Grus japonensis. See Crane, Manchurian
Gull, 58, 64, 77, 116; illus., 114, 129
    Bonaparte's (*Larus philadelphia*), illus.,
    11
    glaucous (*Larus hyperboreus*), 80
    herring (*Larus argentatus*), illus., 89
    laughing (*Larus atricilla*), 21
Gyrfalcon, snow-white (*Falco rusticolus*), 32
Habitat destruction, 135-143
Haematopus. See Oystercatcher
Haliaeetus leucocephalus. See Eagle, bald
Hamilton, W.D., 32, 36-37
Harpia harpyia. See Eagle, harpy
Harrier, northern (*Circus cyaneus*), 66
Harrison, Hal, 25, 26
Hartshorne, Charles, 49, 53
Harvey, Paul, 107
Hawk, 31, 90
    broad-winged (*Buteo platypterus*), illus.,
    23
    Harris's (*Parabuteo unicinctus*), illus., 23
    marsh (*Circus cyaneus*), 66
    sharp-shinned (*Accipiter striatus*), 32;
    illus., 30
Hawk-eagle, ornate (*Spizaetus ornatus*),
    23, 58; illus., 22
Heinrich, Bernd, 99, 103
Heron, 58
    great blue (*Ardea herodias*), 73, 80;

illus., 59, 74, 101
    green (*Butorides virescens*), 93-94; illus.,
    94
    green-backed (*Butorides striatus*), 100
    little blue (*Florida caerulea*), illus., 115
Hesperiphona vespertina. See Grosbeak,
    evening
Hickey, Joseph, 147, 148, 150
Hirundo rustica. See Swallow, barn
Hoatzin (*Opisthocomus hoazin*), 105,
    106-107, 111; illus., 104
Holmes, Richard, 132
Honey guide, 111
Howard, H. Eliot, 147, 152
Hummingbird, 16, 125-127, 132
    broad-tailed (*Selasphorus platycercus*),
    illus., 17
    mountain gem (*Lampornis*), 127
    ruby-throated (*Archilochus colubris*), 16,
    122-123, 139, 142; illus., 124
    rufous (*Selasphorus rufus*), illus.,
    126-127
    violet sabre-wing (*Campylopterus
    hemileucurus*), 127; illus., 124
Hutchinson, G.E., 148
Hylocichla mustelina. See Thrush, wood
Ibis leucocephalus. See Stork, painted
Icterus spp. See Oriole
Image mimicry, 97-103
Intelligence, 105-111
Jacana, American (*Jacana spinosa*), 70-71
Jaeger (*Stercorarius*), 64
Jay, 25, 59, 108, 128, 131
    blue (*Cyanocitta cristata*), 87, 88, 100,
    101-102, 103
    scrub (*Aphelocoma coerulescens*), 113
Jungle fowl, red (*Gallus gallus*), 33
Kamil, Alan, 103, 111
Keeton, William, 44
Kestrel (*Falco*), 37; illus., 36
Kilham, Lawrence, 152-153
Killdeer (*Charadrius vociferus*), 91,
    illus., 90
Kingbird, eastern (*Tyrannus tyrannus*), 139
Kittiwake, 116-118
Klopfer, Peter, 107
Kodrick Brown, Astrid and Jim, 125
Krebs, John, 80
Kroodsma, Donald, 49
Lagopus lagopus. See Ptarmigan, willow
Lampornis. See Hummingbird, mountain
    gem
Lanio versicolor. See Shrike tanager,
    white-winged
Larus spp. See Gull
Lekking, 56, 57, 68-69; illus., 8
Leopold, Aldo, 148
Levins, Richard, 150
Livingston, John A., 133
Lockley, R.M., 111
Loffredo, Christopher, 45-47
Loon (*Gavia*), 52; illus., 52
    common (*Gavia immer*), illus., 67
Lorenz, Konrad, 114
Lorikeet, rainbow (*Trichoglossus
    haematodus*), illus., 39
Loxia. See Crossbill
Luscinia megarhynchos. See Nightingale
Lyon, Bruce, 48, 92, 149
MacArthur, Robert, 127, 148
Macaw, 109
    scarlet (*Ara macao*), illus., 110
Mallard duck (*Anas platyrhynchos*),

illus., 71
Manakin, 45, 69-70
Marler, Peter, 87, 88
Martin, Kathy, 58-64
Martin, purple (*Progne subis*), 113
    sand (*Riparia*), 77
Mason, Russ, 22
Mating systems, 57-71
    and bird song, 45-47, 49
Mayr, Ernst, 148
Meadowlark (*Sturnella*), 65; illus., 53
Melanerpes formicivorus. See Woodpecker,
    acorn
Meleagris gallopavo. See Turkey
Melopsittacus undulatus. See Budgerigar
Melospiza spp. See Sparrow
Migratory birds, illus., 134, 142
    destruction of southern habitat, 135-143
Miller, Richard, 125
Mimicry, 97-103
Mimus polyglottos. See Mockingbird,
    northern
Mindell, David, 107
Mistletoe bird (*Dicaeum hirundinaceum*),
    128
Mockingbird, 49
    northern (*Mimus polyglottos*), illus., 131
Monarch butterfly, 101-103
Monogamy, 57-65
Montgomerie, Bob, 48, 92, 125
Moorhen (*Gallinula*), 70
Morton, Eugene, 47, 52-53, 139
Motmot, illus., 100
    turquoise-browed (*Eumomota
    superciliosa*), 100
Munn, Charles, 90
Murre (*Uria*), 74, 80
    thick-billed (*Uria lomvia*), 80-82; illus.,
    66, 81, 148, 149
Mutualistic relationships, 123-125,
    128-131
    conflicts within, 131-132
Myiarchus spp. See Flycatcher
Myiodynastes luteiventris. See Flycatcher,
    sulphur-bellied
Natural selection, 30. See also Sexual
    selection; Social selection
    and ecological relationships, 132
    and individual reproductive success,
    114-118
Nests, adaptive significance of, 15-26
Nettleship, David, 80
Nice, Margaret Morse, 145-147, 152
Nightingale (*Luscinia megarhynchos*), 43
Nucifraga columbiana. See Nutcracker,
    Clark's
Nutcracker, Clark's (*Nucifraga
    columbiana*), 130, 132; illus., 47
Nuthatch, 38, 128
    red-breasted (*Sitta canadensis*), 24-25
    white-breasted (*Sitta carolinensis*), 25
Nyctea scandiaca. See Owl, snowy
Ogburn, Charlton, 40, 44, 111
Old-squaw duck (*Clangula hyemalis*), 21
Olor buccinator. See Swan, trumpeter
Opisthocomus hoazin. See Hoatzin
Oriole, 21
    Baltimore (*Icterus galbula galbula*), 142
    hooded (*Icterus cucullatus*), illus., 19
    northern (*Icterus galbula*), 18-19
    orchard (*Icterus spurius*), 65
Osprey (*Pandion haliaetus*), 84-85;
    illus., 85

Otus asio. See Owl, screech
Ovenbird (*Seiurus aurocapillus*), 49, 136; illus., 136
Owl, 105, 111
  barred (*Strix varia*), illus., 99
  great grey (*Strix nebulosa*), 131
  great horned (*Bubo virginianus*), 23, 99; illus., 58, 91
  screech (*Otus asio*), illus., 14, 25
  screech, eastern (*Otus asio*), 22-24
  short-eared (*Asio flammeus*), 66
  snowy (*Nyctea scandiaca*), 131
Oxpecker (*Buphagus*), illus., 125
Oystercatcher, 108
  black (*Haematopus bachmani*), illus., 108
Pandion haliaetus. See Osprey
Parabuteo unicinctus. See Hawk, Harris's
Parrot, 38-40, 45, 105, 108
  red-lored (*Amazona autumnalis*), illus., 139
Parus spp. See Chickadee; Titmouse
Passer domesticus. See Sparrow, house
Passerina spp. See Bunting
Peacock (*Pavo cristatus*), illus., 28, 33
Peewee, eastern wood (*Contopus virens*), 139-140
Pelican, brown (*Pelecanus occidentalis*), illus., 12
  great white (*Pelecanus oncrotalus*), 107
  white (*Pelecanus erythrorhynchos*), 116; illus., 106
Penguin, chinstrap (*Pygoscelis antarctica*), illus., 79
  gentoo (*Pygoscelis papua*), illus., 60, 77
  king (*Aptenodytes patagonicus*) illus., 68, 72
Perissocephalus tricolor. See Calf bird, spotted
Peters, Robert, 148
Petrel, 58
Petrochelidon pyrrhonota. See Swallow, cliff
Phainopepla (*Phainopepla nitens*), 128-130; illus., 130
Phalarope (*Phalaropus*), 70
Pharomachrus spp. See Quetzal
Pheasant, 45
Phoebe, 26, 113
  eastern (*Sayornis phoebe*), 21-22, 49
Phoenicopterus ruber. See Flamingo, American
Picoides spp. See Woodpecker
Pigeon, 37
Piranga olivacea. See Tanager, scarlet
Plectrophenax nivalis. See Bunting, snow
Plumage, beauty in, 29-33, 36-41
Podiceps grisegena. See Grebe, red-necked
Polyandry, 70-71
Polygyny, 65-69
Procnias tricarunculata. See Bellbird, three-wattled
Progne subis. See Martin, purple
Protonotaria citrea. See Warbler, prothonotary
Ptarmigan, willow (*Lagopus lagopus*), 58-64; illus., 61
Ptilonorhynchus violaceus. See Bowerbird, satin
Puffin, 77-80, 111; illus., 76-77
  Atlantic (*Fratercula arctica*), illus., 95
Puffinus. See Shearwater
Pygoscelis spp. See Penguin
Pyrocephalus rubinus. See Flycatcher, vermilion

Quetzal (*Pharomachrus*), illus., 133
  resplendent (*Pharomachrus mocino*), 70, 130
Quiscalus major. See Grackle, boat-tailed
Ramphastos spp. See Toucan
Raptors, 58, 65, 109, 111, 116
Raven (*Corvus corax*), 58, 64, 105; illus., 128
Read, Andrew, 37
Redpoll (*Acanthis flammea*), 131
Reproductive success and competition, 114-118
Riparia. See Martin, sand
Robertson, Raleigh, 21, 40, 114
Robin (*Turdus migratorius*), 111, 152
Robinson, Scott, 66-68
Rohwer, Seifert, 92
Rooster, 44, 47, 91
Rothschild, Miriam, 77
Rubinoff, Roberta, 100
Rupicola rupicola. See Cock-of-the-rock, Guianan
Russell, Franklin, 74
Sandpiper, 45, 70
Sapsucker, yellow-bellied (*Sphyrapicus varius*), 152
Sarcorhamphus papa. See Vulture, king
Sayornis phoebe. See Phoebe, eastern
Seabirds, 40, 65, 74, 116
Seiurus aurocapillus. See Ovenbird
Selander, R.K., 31
Selasphorus spp. See Hummingbird
Serinus canaria. See Canary
Sexual selection and beauty, 30-38
Shag, blue-eyed (*Phalacrocorax atriceps*), illus., 67
Shearwater (*Puffinus*), 57, 58
Sherry, Tom, 132
Short, Lester, 140
Shrike, 51
Shrike tanager, white-winged (*Lanio versicolor*), 90-91
Sialia. See Bluebird
Siskin, pine (*Carduelis pinus*), 131
Sitta. See Nuthatch
Skua, 77-80; illus., 77
Smith, John, 87
Smith, Susan, 65, 100
Snipe, 70
Social selection and beauty, 38-40
Social systems and intelligence, 108
Solitaire, 53
Song, purpose and value of, 43-53
Sparrow, 49, 116
  Harris's (*Zonotrichia querula*), 92
  house (*Passer domesticus*), 24
  song (*Melospiza melodia*), 49, 51, 65, 108, 145, 147
  swamp (*Melospiza georgiana*), 51, 108; illus., 51, 109
  white-throated (*Zonotrichia albicollis*), 52
Sphyrapicus varius. See Sapsucker, yellow-bellied
Spizaetus ornatus. See Hawk-eagle, ornate
Starling (*Sturnus vulgaris*), 22, 49
Stercorarius. See Jaeger
Sterna paradisaea. See Tern, Arctic
Stork, 58
  Asian open-bill (*Anastomus oscitans*), illus., 62
  painted (*Ibis leucocephalus*), illus., 83
Stresemann, Erwin, 147
Strix spp. See Owl

Sturnella. See Meadowlark
Sturnus vulgaris. See Starling
Stutchbury, Bridget, 40
Sula bassana. See Gannet
Sullivan, Kimberly, 89
Sunbittern (*Eurypyga helias*), 97-99; illus., 98
Swallow, 18
  barn (*Hirundo rustica*), 15-16
  cliff (*Petrochelidon pyrrhonota*), 77, 82-84; illus., 17, 82
  tree (*Tachycineta bicolor*), 25, 40, 58, 65, 113, 114
Swan, trumpeter (*Olor buccinator*), illus., 10, 116-117
Swift, black (*Cypseloides niger*), 18
  cave, 18
  chimney (*Chaetura pelagica*), 18
  common (*Apus apus*), 18
  palm (*Cypsiurus parvus*), 18
  white-throated (*Aeronautes saxatalis*), 18
Symbolism in bird communication, 91-94
Tachycineta bicolor. See Swallow, tree
Tanager, 40
  scarlet (*Piranga olivacea*), 29, 31, 41, 92, 139
  white-winged shrike (*Lanio versicolor*), 90-91
Terborgh, John, 90, 141, 143
Tern, 80
  Arctic (*Sterna paradisaea*), 21; illus., 20, 59
  elegant (*Thalasseus elegans*), illus., 80
  royal (*Thalasseus maximus*), illus., 76, 117
Thalasseus spp. See Tern
Thamnomanes schistogynus. See Antshrike, bluish-slate
Thomas, Lewis, 122
Thrasher, brown, 49
Thrush, hermit (*Catharus guttatus*), 43-44, 53
  Swainson's (*Catharus ustulatus*), 44
  wood (*Hylocichla mustelina*), 44
Tit, English, 109
Titmouse, tufted (*Parus bicolor*), 25-26, 89-90
Toucan, 38-40
  chestnut-mandibled (*Ramphastos swainsonii*), 107-108
  Cuvier's (*Ramphastos cuvieri*), 68
Toucanet, emerald (*Aulacorhynchus prasinus*), illus., 38
Trail, Pepper, 69
Trichoglossus haematodus. See Lorikeet, rainbow
Troglodytes aedon. See Wren, house
Tropical forest, destruction of, 135-143
Turdus migratorius. See Robin
Turkey (*Meleagris gallopavo*), 47, 105
  domestic, 119; illus., 118
  wild, 119; illus., 119
Tympanuchus spp. See Chicken, prairie; Grouse
Tyrannus tyrannus. See Kingbird, eastern
Umbrella bird, 49
  bare-necked (*Cephalopterus glabricollis*), 47
Uria spp. See Murre
Vehrencamp, Sandra, 115
Vermivora peregrina. See Warbler, Tennessee
Viceroy butterfly, 102-103

Violence among birds, 113-119
Vireo, 53
  grey (*Vireo vicinior*), 139
  Philadelphia (*Vireo philadelphicus*), 139, 142
  red-eyed (*Vireo olivaceus*), 139
Vultur gryphus. See Condor, Andean
Vulture, black (*Coragyps atratus*), 133
  king (*Sarcorhamphus papa*), illus., 41
  turkey (*Cathartes aura*), 121-122, 133; illus., 120, 122
Wake Robin, by John Burroughs, 147
Wallace, Alfred Russell, 33
Warbler, 111, 127, 141, 142
  blackpoll (*Dendroica striata*), 65, 135
  Cape May (*Dendroica tigrina*), illus., 143
  Christmas Island, 152
  prothonotary (*Protonotaria citrea*), illus., 140
  Tennessee (*Vermivora peregrina*), 135
  yellow (*Dendroica petechia*), 21; illus., 20
Ward, Peter, 80
Waterfowl, migratory, illus., 142
Watt, Doris, 92
Weaver, 45
  grosbeak (*Amblyospiza albifrons*), illus., 19
West-Eberhard, Mary Jane, 38
Wildlife, value of, 122, 133
Wilson, E.O., 41, 88
Woodpecker, 38, 105, 109
  acorn (*Melanerpes formicivorus*), 113
  downy (*Picoides pubescens*), 52, 89, 128, 152-153
  hairy (*Picoides villosus*), 52, 128, 152
  pileated (*Dryocopus pileatus*), 152-153; illus., 24
  red-cockaded (*Picoides borealis*), 24
Wren, 49, 51
  house (*Troglodytes aedon*), 113; illus., 42
  marsh (*Cistothorus palustris*), 49, illus., 48, 88
  rufous-naped, 51-52
  sedge (*Cistothorus platensis*), illus., 49
  short-billed marsh (*Cistothorus platensis*) illus., 49
Xanthocephalus xanthocephalus. See Blackbird, yellow-headed
Zahavi, Amotz, 80
Zenaida asiatica. See Dove, white-winged
Zonotrichia spp. See Sparrow
Zuk, Marlene, 36-37

CREDITS

The following contributors are gratefully acknowledged: p. 6 Wendell D. Metzen/Bruce Coleman Inc.; p. 8 Tim Fitzharris; p. 10 Michael S. Quinton; p. 11 Tim Fitzharris; p. 12 (top) Leonard Rue Jr./DRK Photo, (bottom) Alan D. Carey; p. 13 William Ervin; p. 14 John Bova/Photo Researchers, Inc.; p. 17 (top) Stephen J. Krasemann/DRK Photo, (bottom) Leonard Rue Jr./Photo Researchers, Inc.; p. 18 Michael S. Quinton; p. 19 (left) Wayne Lankinen, (right) Stephen J. Krasemann/DRK Photo; p. 20 (top) Stephen J. Krasemann/DRK Photo, (bottom) Keith N. Logan; p. 21 Jeff March/Tom Stack & Associates; p. 22 Bruce Lyon; p. 23 (top) Tim Fitzharris, (bottom) Wayne Lankinen; p. 24 Wayne Lankinen; p. 25 Robert C. Simpson/Valan Photos; p. 26 Michael H. Francis; p. 27 C. Allan Morgan/DRK Photo; p. 28 Wayne Lynch; p. 30 Mike Blair; p. 31 L. West/Photo Researchers, Inc.; p. 32 Robert Villani; p. 33 D. Cavasnaro/DRK Photo; p. 34 Frithfoto/Bruce Coleman Inc.; p. 35 M.P. Kahl/Bruce Coleman Inc.; p. 36 James D. Markou; p. 37 James M. Richards; p. 38 Bruce Lyon; p. 39 Stephen J. Krasemann/DRK Photo; p. 40 Wolfgang Kaehler; p. 41 Wilf Schurig; p. 42 Tim Fitzharris; p. 44 Jeff Foott; p. 45 Stephen J. Krasemann/DRK Photo; p. 46 Jerry L. Ferrara; p. 47 Don Johnston/Photo/Nats; p. 48 Tom Mangelsen; p. 49 James R. Fisher/DRK Photo; p. 50 J.R. Page/Valan Photos; p. 51 Robert McCaw; p. 52 Tom Mangelsen; p. 53 Phil Farnes/Photo Researchers, Inc.; p. 54 Alan D. Carey; p. 56 Wilf Schurig; p. 57 Robert W. Hernandez/Photo Researchers, Inc.; p. 58 Keith N. Logan; p. 59 (top) Michael S. Quinton, (bottom) Albert Kuhnigk; p. 60 Wolfgang Kaehler; p. 61 Erwin & Peggy Bauer/Bruce Coleman Inc.; p. 62-63 (left) Michael Freeman/Bruce Coleman Inc., (right) John Eastcott/Yva Momatiuk; p. 64 John Eastcott/Yva Momatiuk; p. 65 Michael S. Quinton; p. 66 Bruce Lyon; p. 67 (top) Tom W. Parkin/Pathfinder, (bottom) Wolfgang Kaehler; p. 68 Frans Lanting; p. 69 Mike Blair; p. 70 C.C. Lockwood/DRK Photo; p. 71 Tom W. Parkin/Pathfinder; p. 72 George Holton/Photo Researchers, Inc.; p. 74 Cameron Davidson/Bruce Coleman Inc.; p. 75 John Eastcott/Yva Momatiuk; p. 76 (top) John Eastcott/Yva Momatiuk, (bottom) Bruce Lyon; p. 77 Wolfgang Kaehler; p. 78-79 (left) Bruce Lyon, (right) Wolfgang Kaehler; p. 80 Gerald Corsi/Tom Stack & Associates; p. 81 (top) C.C. Lockwood/DRK Photo, (bottom) Bruce Lyon/Valan Photos; p. 82 Tom Mangelsen; p. 83 Mike Price/Bruce Coleman Inc.; p. 84 William Ervin; p. 85 Bruce Milne/Animals Animals; p. 86 William Ervin; p. 88 Tom Mangelsen; p. 89 John Eastcott/Yva Momatiuk; p. 90 Bruce Lyon; p. 91 Albert Kuhnigk; p. 93 Jeff Lepore/Photo Researchers, Inc.; p. 94 Tim Fitzharris; p. 95 Robert Villani; p. 96 John Gerlach/Animals Animals; p. 98 (top) Bruce Lyon, (bottom) J.H. Robinson/Photo Researchers, Inc.; p. 99 Francis Lépine; p. 100 Carol Hughes/Bruce Coleman Inc.; p. 101 Alan D. Carey; p. 102 Michael Fogden/Animals Animals; p. 104 Sullivan & Rogers/Bruce Coleman Inc.; p. 106 Leonard Rue Jr./Bruce Coleman Inc.; p. 107 E.P.I. Nancy Adams/Tom Stack & Associates; p. 108 Tim Fitzharris; p. 109 Robert McCaw; p. 110 (top) L. & D. Klein/Photo Researchers, Inc., (bottom) Frans Lanting; p. 112 Mike Blair; p. 114 John Eastcott/Yva Momatiuk; p. 115 Erwin & Peggy Bauer; p. 116 Alan D. Carey; p. 117 (top) Mary Clay/Tom Stack & Associates, (bottom) Albert Kuhnigk; p. 118 Phil Degginger/Bruce Coleman Inc.; p. 119 Phil Farnes/Photo Researchers, Inc.; p. 120 Jen & Des Bartlett/Bruce Coleman Inc.; p. 122 Jerry L. Ferrara; p. 123 Frans Lanting; p. 124 (top) Wayne Lankinen/Valan Photos, (bottom) Bruce Lyon; p. 125 Stephen J. Krasemann /DRK Photo; p. 126 Michael S. Quinton; p. 127 Tim Fitzharris; p. 128 Tim Fitzharris; p. 129 Alan Detrick; p. 130 Jeff Foott; p. 131 Joe McDonald/Bruce Coleman Inc.; p. 132 William Ervin; p. 133 Bruce Lyon; p. 134 Robert McCaw; p. 136 Keith N. Logan; p. 137 (top) William Grenfell, (bottom) Verna R. Johnston/Photo Researchers, Inc.; p. 138 Erwin & Peggy Bauer/Bruce Coleman Inc.; p. 139 Bruce Lyon; p. 140 Pam Hickman/Valan Photos; p. 141 Y.R. Tymstra/Valan Photos; p. 142 Jeff Foott/Tom Stack & Associates; p. 143 Jack Wilburn; p. 144 Francis Lépine; p. 146 (top) Robert Villani, (bottom) Stephen J. Krasemann/DRK Photo; p. 148 Bruce Lyon; p. 149 Bruce Lyon; p. 151 (top) Robert P. Carr/Bruce Coleman Inc., (bottom) Arthur Morris; p. 152 W. & E.A. Schreiber/Animals Animals; p. 153 Stephen J. Krasemann/DRK Photo; p. 154 M. Philip Kahl Jr./DRK Photo